# Microsoft® Office Access 2003

## Level 3

Christopher J. Worden

# Microsoft® Office Access 2003: Level 3

Part Number: 084462
Course Edition: 1.1

## ACKNOWLEDGMENTS

### *Project Team*

**Content Developer:** Christopher J. Worden and Thomas R. Stone • **Content Manager:** Cheryl Russo • **Content Editors:** Cory Brown, Christy D. Johnson and Margaux Phillips • **Material Editor:** Frank Wosnick • **Graphic/Print Designer:** Julie Popken • **Project Technical Support:** Michael Toscano

## NOTICES

**DISCLAIMER:** While Element K Content LLC takes care to ensure the accuracy and quality of these materials, we cannot guarantee their accuracy, and all materials are provided without any warranty whatsoever, including, but not limited to, the implied warranties of merchantability or fitness for a particular purpose. The name used in the data files for this course is that of a fictitious company. Any resemblance to current or future companies is purely coincidental. We do not believe we have used anyone's name in creating this course, but if we have, please notify us and we will change the name in the next revision of the course. Element K is an independent provider of integrated training solutions for individuals, businesses, educational institutions, and government agencies. Use of screenshots, photographs of another entity's products, or another entity's product name or service in this book is for editorial purposes only. No such use should be construed to imply sponsorship or endorsement of the book by, nor any affiliation of such entity with Element K. This courseware may contain links to sites on the Internet that are owned and operated by third parties (the "External Sites"). Element K is not responsible for the availability of, or the content located on or through, any External Site. Please contact Element K if you have any concerns regarding such links or External Sites.

**TRADEMARK NOTICES** Element K and the Element K logo are trademarks of Element K LLC and its affiliates.

Microsoft® Office Access 2003 is a registered trademark of Microsoft Corporation in the U.S. and other countries; the Microsoft Corporation products and services discussed or described may be trademarks of Microsoft Corporation . All other product names and services used throughout this course may be common law or registered trademarks of their respective proprietors.

Copyright © 2006 Element K Content LLC. All rights reserved. Screenshots used for illustrative purposes are the property of the software proprietor. This publication, or any part thereof, may not be reproduced or transmitted in any form or by any means, electronic or mechanical, including photocopying, recording, storage in an information retrieval system, or otherwise, without express written permission of Element K, 500 Canal View Boulevard, Rochester, NY 14623, (585) 240-7500, (800) 434-3466. Element K Courseware LLC's World Wide Web site is located at www.elementkcourseware.com.

This book conveys no rights in the software or other products about which it was written; all use or licensing of such software or other products is the responsibility of the user according to terms and conditions of the owner. Do not make illegal copies of books or software. If you believe that this book, related materials, or any other Element K materials are being reproduced or transmitted without permission, please call 1-800-478-7788.

HELP US IMPROVE OUR COURSEWARE

Your comments are important to us. Please contact us at Element K Press LLC, 1-800-478-7788, 500 Canal View Boulevard, Rochester, NY 14623, Attention: Product Planning, or through our Web site at http://support.elementkcourseware.com.

**Microsoft® Office Specialist — Approved Courseware**

This logo means that this courseware has been approved by the Microsoft® Office Specialist Program to be among the finest available for learning Microsoft Access 2003. It also means that upon completion of this courseware, you may be prepared to take an exam for Microsoft Offices Specialist qualification.

What is a Microsoft Office Specialist? A Microsoft Office Specialist is an individual who has passed exams for certifying his or her skills in one or more of the Microsoft Office desktop applications such as Microsoft Word, Microsoft Excel, Microsoft PowerPoint, Microsoft Outlook, Microsoft Access, or Microsoft Project. The Microsoft Office Specialist Program typically offers certification exams at the "Core" and "Expert" skill levels. The Microsoft Office Specialist Program is the only program in the world approved by Microsoft for testing proficiency in Microsoft Office desktop applications and Microsoft Project. This testing program can be a valuable asset in any job search or career advancement.

To learn more about becoming a Microsoft Office Specialist, visit **www.microsoft.com/officespecialist**. To learn more about other Microsoft Office Specialist approved courseware from Element K, visit **www.elementkcourseware.com**.

*The availability of Microsoft Office Specialist certification exams varies by application, application version, and language. Visit **www.microsoft.com/officespecialist** for exam availability.

Microsoft, the Microsoft Office Logo, PowerPoint, and Outlook are trademarks or registered trademarks of Microsoft Corporation in the United States and/or other countries, and the Microsoft Office Specialist Logo is used under license from owner.

Element K is independent from Microsoft Corporation, and not affiliated with Microsoft in any manner. This publication may be used in assisting students to prepare for a Microsoft Office Specialist exam. Neither Microsoft, its designated program administrator or courseware reviewer, nor Element K warrants that use of this publication will ensure passing the relevant exam.

# NOTES

# MICROSOFT® OFFICE ACCESS 2003: LEVEL 3

## CONTENTS

### LESSON 1: STRUCTURING EXISTING DATA

A. Import Data .................................................. 2
    Imported Data ............................................ 2
B. Analyze Tables .............................................. 5
    Table Analyzer Wizard ................................... 5
C. Create a Junction Table ................................... 10
    Many-to-Many Relationships ............................ 10
    Junction Tables ......................................... 10
D. Improve Table Structure .................................. 13

### LESSON 2: WRITING ADVANCED QUERIES

A. Create Unmatched and Duplicates Queries ............... 20
B. Group and Summarize Records Using the Criteria Field . 23
    The Criteria Field ...................................... 23
C. Summarize Data with a Crosstab Query ................. 27
    Crosstab Query ......................................... 27
D. Create a PivotTable and a PivotChart .................. 32
    PivotTable .............................................. 32
    PivotChart .............................................. 32
E. Display a Graphical Summary on a Form ................ 39

### LESSON 3: SIMPLIFYING TASKS WITH MACROS

A. Create a Macro ............................................ 46
    Macros .................................................. 46
    The Macro Window ..................................... 46

# Contents

    **B. Attach a Macro to a Command Button** .............................. 50

        Object Events ............................................................ 50

    **C. Restrict Records Using a Where Condition** ........................ 53

        The Where Condition ................................................. 53

## Lesson 4: Adding Interaction and Automation with Macros

    **A. Require Data Entry with a Macro** .................................... 58

        Macro Conditions ...................................................... 58

        Validating Data with Macros ...................................... 58

        Plan a Macro ............................................................ 59

    **B. Display a Message Box with a Macro** ............................. 66

    **C. Automate Data Entry** ................................................... 68

## Lesson 5: Making Forms More Effective

    **A. Change the Display of Data Conditionally** ....................... 76

        Conditional Formatting .............................................. 76

    **B. Display a Calendar on a Form** ....................................... 79

    **C. Organize Information with Tab Pages** ............................. 85

        Tab Pages ................................................................ 85

## Lesson 6: Making Reports More Effective

    **A. Cancel Printing of a Blank Report** .................................. 92

    **B. Include a Chart in a Report** ........................................... 95

    **C. Arrange Data in Columns** ............................................. 98

    **D. Create a Report Snapshot** ........................................... 103

        Report Snapshot ..................................................... 103

        Snapshot Viewer .................................................... 104

## Lesson 7: Maintaining an Access Database

    **A. Link Tables to External Data Sources** ............................. 108

        Linking a File .......................................................... 108

| | |
|---|---|
| B. Back Up a Database | 110 |
| C. Compact and Repair a Database | 112 |
| D. Protect a Database with a Password | 113 |
| E. Determine Object Dependency | 116 |
|     Object Dependency Task Pane | 116 |
| F. Document a Database | 118 |
|     Database Documenter | 118 |
| G. Analyze the Performance of a Database | 120 |
|     Performance Analyzer | 120 |

# APPENDIX A: MICROSOFT OFFICE SPECIALIST PROGRAM

# LESSON LABS ................................................. 127

# SOLUTIONS ................................................... 135

# GLOSSARY .................................................... 141

# INDEX ........................................................ 143

# NOTES

# ABOUT THIS COURSE

Your training in and use of Microsoft® Office Access 2003 has provided you with a solid foundation in the basic and intermediate skills for working in Microsoft® Office Access 2003. You're now ready to extend your knowledge into some of the more specialized and advanced capabilities.

Your basic knowledge of Microsoft® Office Access 2003 to this point allows you to create simple, functional databases. By further exploring Microsoft® Office Access 2003's advanced features, you can take that simple database and turn it into a robust, highly functional one. The results will not only be a joy for the users to work with, but will make your job much easier.

## Course Description

### Target Student

This course is designed for the student who wishes to learn intermediate and advanced operations of the Microsoft® Office Access 2003 database program. The Level 3 course is for the individual whose job responsibilities include working with heavily related tables; creating advanced queries, forms, and reports; writing macros to automate common tasks; and performing general database maintenance. It is also designed as one in a series of courses for students pursuing the Microsoft® Office Specialist Certification for Microsoft® Office Access 2003, and it is a prerequisite to taking more advanced courses in Microsoft® Office Access 2003.

### Course Prerequisites

To ensure the successful completion of *Microsoft® Office Access 2003: Level 3*, we recommend completion of the following Element K courses, or equivalent knowledge (familiarity with basic and intermediate features of Access tables, relationships, queries, forms, and reports) from another source:

- *Microsoft® Office Access 2003: Level 1*
- *Microsoft® Office Access 2003: Level 2*

# INTRODUCTION

# How to Use This Book

## As a Learning Guide

Each lesson covers one broad topic or set of related topics. Lessons are arranged in order of increasing proficiency with *Microsoft® Access 2003*; skills you acquire in one lesson are used and developed in subsequent lessons. For this reason, you should work through the lessons in sequence.

We organized each lesson into results-oriented topics. Topics include all the relevant and supporting information you need to master *Microsoft® Access 2003*, and activities allow you to apply this information to practical hands-on examples.

You get to try out each new skill on a specially prepared sample file. This saves you typing time and allows you to concentrate on the skill at hand. Through the use of sample files, hands-on activities, illustrations that give you feedback at crucial steps, and supporting background information, this book provides you with the foundation and structure to learn *Microsoft® Access 2003* quickly and easily.

## As a Review Tool

Any method of instruction is only as effective as the time and effort you are willing to invest in it. In addition, some of the information that you learn in class may not be important to you immediately, but it may become important later on. For this reason, we encourage you to spend some time reviewing the topics and activities after the course. For additional challenge when reviewing activities, try the "What You Do" column before looking at the "How You Do It" column.

## As a Reference

The organization and layout of the book make it easy to use as a learning tool and as an after-class reference. You can use this book as a first source for definitions of terms, background information on given topics, and summaries of procedures.

# Course Objectives

In this course, you will create complex Access databases using forms, reports, and macros.

You will:

- restructure an existing set of data to improve the design of a database.
- use a variety of techniques to summarize and present data with queries.
- create and revise basic Access macros.
- create macros that improve data entry efficiency and integrity.
- improve the effectiveness of data entry in forms.
- improve the effectiveness of data displayed in reports.
- maintain an Access database by using various utility tools.

# Course Requirements

## Hardware

For this course, you will need one computer for each student and one for the instructor. Each computer will need the following minimum hardware components:

- A 233 MHz Pentium-class processor if you use Windows XP Professional as your operating system. 300 MHz is recommended.
- A 133 MHz Pentium-class processor if you use Windows 2000 Professional as your operating system.
- 128 MB of RAM.
- A 5 GB hard disk or larger if you use Windows XP Professional as your operating system. You should have at least 600 MB of free hard-disk space available for the Office installation.
- A 3 GB hard disk or larger if you use Windows 2000 Professional as your operating system. You should have at least 600 MB of free hard-disk space available for the Office installation.
- A floppy-disk drive.
- A mouse or other pointing device.
- An 800 x 600 resolution monitor.
- Network cards and cabling for local network access.
- Internet access (see your local network administrator).
- A printer (optional).
- A projection system to display the instructor's computer screen.

## Software

- Either Windows XP Professional with Service Pack 1, or Windows 2000 Professional with Service Pack 3.
- Microsoft® Office Professional Edition 2003.

# Class Setup

## For Initial Class Setup

1. Install Windows 2000 Professional or Windows XP Professional on an empty partition.
   - Leave the Administrator password blank.
   - For all other installation parameters, use values that are appropriate for your environment (see your local network administrator if you need details).
2. On Windows 2000 Professional, when the Network Identification Wizard runs after installation, select the option Users Must Enter A User Name And Password To Use This Computer. (This step ensures that students will be able to log on as the Administrator user regardless of what other user accounts exist on the computer.)

*Introduction*

# Introduction

3. On Windows 2000 Professional, in the Getting Started With Windows 2000 window, uncheck Show This Screen At Startup. Click Exit.
4. On Windows 2000 Professional, set 800 x 600 display resolution: Right-click the desktop and choose Properties. Select the Settings tab. Move the Screen Area slider to 800 By 600 Pixels. Click OK twice, and then click Yes.
5. On Windows 2000 Professional, install Service Pack 3. Use the Service Pack installation defaults.
6. On Windows XP Professional, disable the Welcome screen. (This step ensures that students will be able to log on as the Administrator user regardless of what other user accounts exist on the computer.) Click Start and choose Control Panel→User Accounts. Click Change The Way Users Log On And Off. Uncheck Use Welcome Screen. Click Apply Options.
7. On Windows XP Professional, install Service Pack 1. Use the Service Pack installation defaults.
8. On either operating system, install a printer driver (a physical print device is optional).
   — For Windows XP Professional, click Start and choose Printers And Faxes. Under Printer Tasks, click Add A Printer and follow the prompts.
   — For Windows 2000 Professional, click Start and choose Settings→Printers. Run the Add Printer Wizard and follow the prompts.
9. Run the Internet Connection Wizard to set up the Internet connection as appropriate for your environment, if you did not do so during installation.
10. Log on to the computer as the Administrator user if you have not already done so.
11. Perform a Complete installation of Microsoft Office Professional Edition 2003.
12. Minimize the Language Bar if it appears.
13. On the course CD-ROM, open the 084_462 folder. Then, open the Data folder. Run the 084462dd.exe self-extracting file located within. This will install a folder named 084462Data on your C drive. This folder contains all the data files you will use to complete this course.
14. Copy or move the data files to the Administrator user's My Documents folder.
15. On Windows 2000 Professional, remove the Read-only attribute on the downloaded files.
16. With Access open, choose Tools→Macro→Security and set the security level to low.

## Before Every Class

1. Log on to the computer as the Administrator user.
2. Delete any existing data files from the My Documents folder.
3. Extract a fresh copy of the course data files from the CD-ROM provided with the course manual.

## List of Additional Files

Printed with each activity is a list of files students open to complete that activity. Many activities also require additional files that students do not open, but are needed to support the file(s) students are working with. These supporting files are included with the student data files on the course CD-ROM or data disk. Do not delete these files.

# LESSON 1
# Structuring Existing Data

**Lesson Time**
1 hour(s), 20 minutes

## Lesson Objectives:

In this lesson, you will restructure an existing set of data to improve the design of a database. You will:

- Import data as tables from external data sources.
- Use the Table Analyzer Wizard to help you decide on the tables needed to hold your data.
- Create a junction table to eliminate the need for a many-to-many relationship.
- Modify the structure of a set of tables to meet a target design structure.

# LESSON 1

## Introduction

As an advanced-level Microsoft® Office Access 2003 user, you may be in the position of having to straighten out databases that less knowledgeable users have created. Or, you may inherit data originally kept in some other program and need to figure out how to implement that data in Access. This lesson shows you how to do that.

Being able to identify and resolve problems with the design of tables will assist you in troubleshooting databases. Knowing the most efficient way to get existing data into properly designed Access tables will save enormous amounts of time in data entry.

# TOPIC A

# Import Data

As you manage your databases, you may find that some of the data you want to include in your database has been stored in another database or even another program. In this topic, you will learn how to expand the power of Access by calling on data outside of your own database.

Perhaps, unfortunately, your co-workers are not using Access as their master information storage resource. Because of this, it is possible that the data you need resides in a spreadsheet or a text file. In those cases, you'll need to bend a little and make the best of the situation. If you can successfully import data from other applications, then your world knows no bounds. Getting that data into your database can be a snap, and then working with that data is no different than what you're used to.

## Imported Data

### Definition:

*Imported data* is external information that can be brought into and used in an Access database. The data must be structured in such a way that Access can understand and break down the information into a *table*. Imported data can come from many different sources, for example, a table from another Access database, Microsoft® Office Excel, or a comma delimited text file.

### Example:

One of the most common types of imported data is from an Excel spreadsheet.

# LESSON 1

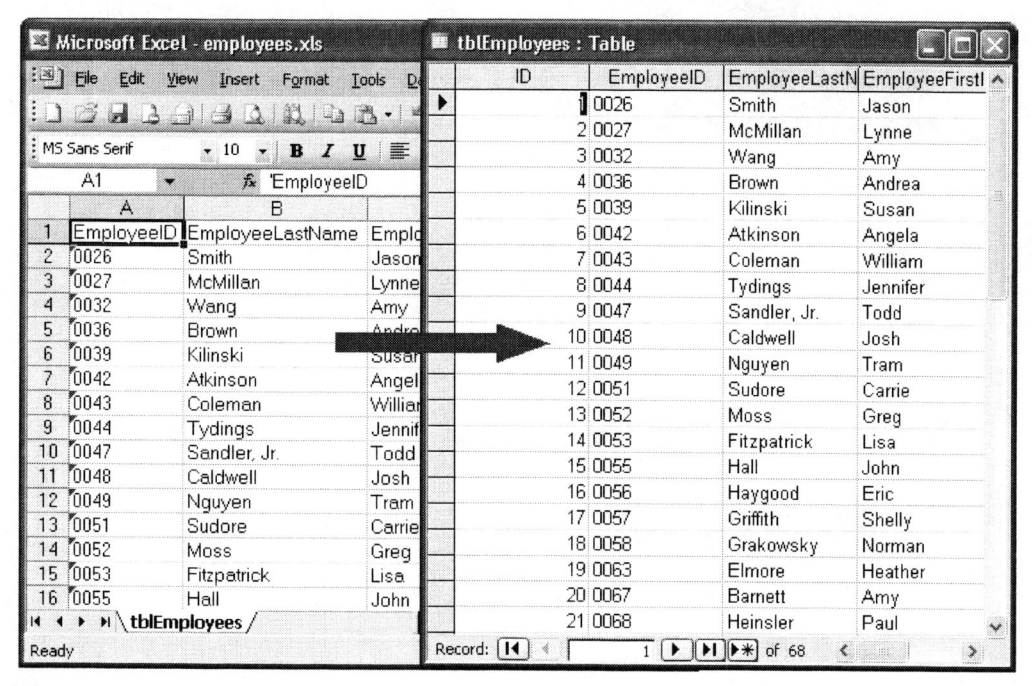

**Figure 1-1:** *Importing data from Excel to Access.*

# How to Import Data

## Procedure Reference: Import Data

To import data:

1. With Access already open, choose File→Get External Data→Import.

2. From the Files Of Type drop-down list, select the correct file type.

3. Navigate to the file you want to import from and double-click it.

4. Follow any prompts to customize the import.

# LESSON 1

# ACTIVITY 1-1

## Importing Data

**Data Files:**

- Employees.xls
- Projects.mdb

**Scenario:**

One of your co-workers has come to you for some help. She has an existing database and a text file that she needs to get into one combined database. You offer to help.

| What You Do | How You Do It |
|---|---|
| 1. In a new database called myImports.mdb, **import tblProjects from Projects.mdb.** | a. With Access already open, **choose File→New.** |
| | b. From the task pane, **choose Blank Database.** |
| | c. **Navigate to the My Documents folder. Name the database myImports.mdb and click Create.** |
| | d. **Choose File→Get External Data→Import.** |
| | e. **Verify that Files Of Type is set to Microsoft Office Access. Navigate to the My Documents folder and double-click Projects.mdb.** |
| | f. From the Import Objects window, **select tblProjects and click OK.** |

# Lesson 1

2. Import the data from Employees.xls into a new table titled tblEmployees.

   a. Choose File→Get External Data→Import.

   b. Change the Files Of Type to Microsoft Excel.

   c. Double-click Employees.xls.

   d. Click Next to advance past the first screen of the wizard.

   e. Check the First Row Contains Column Headings check box. Click Next.

   f. Click Next to store the data in a new table.

   g. Click Next to advance the wizard.

   h. Select the No Primary Key option and click Next.

   i. Accept the default name and click Finish to create the table.

   j. Click OK at the message box.

# TOPIC B

# Analyze Tables

You've created tables from scratch and by using a wizard, but, in those cases, you didn't have existing data to deal with. The Table Analyzer Wizard is an Access tool that can help you create new tables from an improperly designed table that already contains data.

If you use the Table Analyzer Wizard to create new tables, the Analyzer will move the existing data for you. This saves you time in having to write queries, or in data entry, to transfer the data from the old table structure to the new.

## Table Analyzer Wizard

The *Table Analyzer Wizard* will help you manage existing Access data. The wizard will examine an existing database and make suggestions as to how to make the database run more efficiently. If you accept the suggestions given by the wizard, it will perform many of the tasks for you.

*Lesson 1: Structuring Existing Data*

# LESSON 1

## How to Analyze Tables

**Procedure Reference: Use the Table Analyzer Wizard**

To use the Table Analyzer Wizard:

1. Open the database containing the table you want to check.
2. Choose Tools→Analyze→Table.
3. The first dialog box explains the problems caused by repeating information. When you're ready, click Next to move on.
4. The next dialog box explains how Access will solve the problem. Click Next to continue.
5. From the table list, select the table you want the wizard to analyze. Click Next.
6. Choose the Yes, Let The Wizard Decide option. Click Next.
7. Rename the corrected tables. Click Next.
8. Confirm the primary keys. Click Next.
9. Choose the No, Don't Create The Query option.
10. Click Finish.

# ACTIVITY 1-2

## Running the Table Analyzer Wizard

**Data Files:**

- Structure.mdb

**Scenario:**

You're an information analyst with Lone Pine Outfitters, a wholesaler of camping equipment. You've just joined the company and part of your new job is to support Access users and help ensure the integrity of the data being used around the company. The sales manager asks you to look at the table he's been using to track orders since he knows it contains redundant data. In an effort to save time, you've decided to try using the Table Analyzer Wizard to redesign the table and move the existing data.

| What You Do | How You Do It |
| --- | --- |
| 1. In Structure.mdb, **open the LonePineSales table.** | a. In Structure.mdb, **double-click the LonePineSales table.** |

2. What is the major problem with the data caused by a poor table design?

3. What is the cause of these problems?

_____

4. What is the cure for these problems?

_____

5. Run the Table Analyzer Wizard to the point where the data has been grouped into tables. Arrange the tables so that all five are visible at once.

   📌 In Windows 2000 Professional, you have to remove the Read-only attribute on a file to run the Table Analyzer Wizard.

   a. Close the table.

   b. Choose Tools→Analyze→Table.

   c. Click Next.

   d. Click Next.

   e. In the Tables list, **verify that LonePineSales is selected and click Next.**

   f. Verify that Yes, Let The Wizard Decide is selected and click Next.

   g. Using the title bars, **drag the tables so that all five are visible at once.**

*Lesson 1: Structuring Existing Data*

# LESSON 1

6.

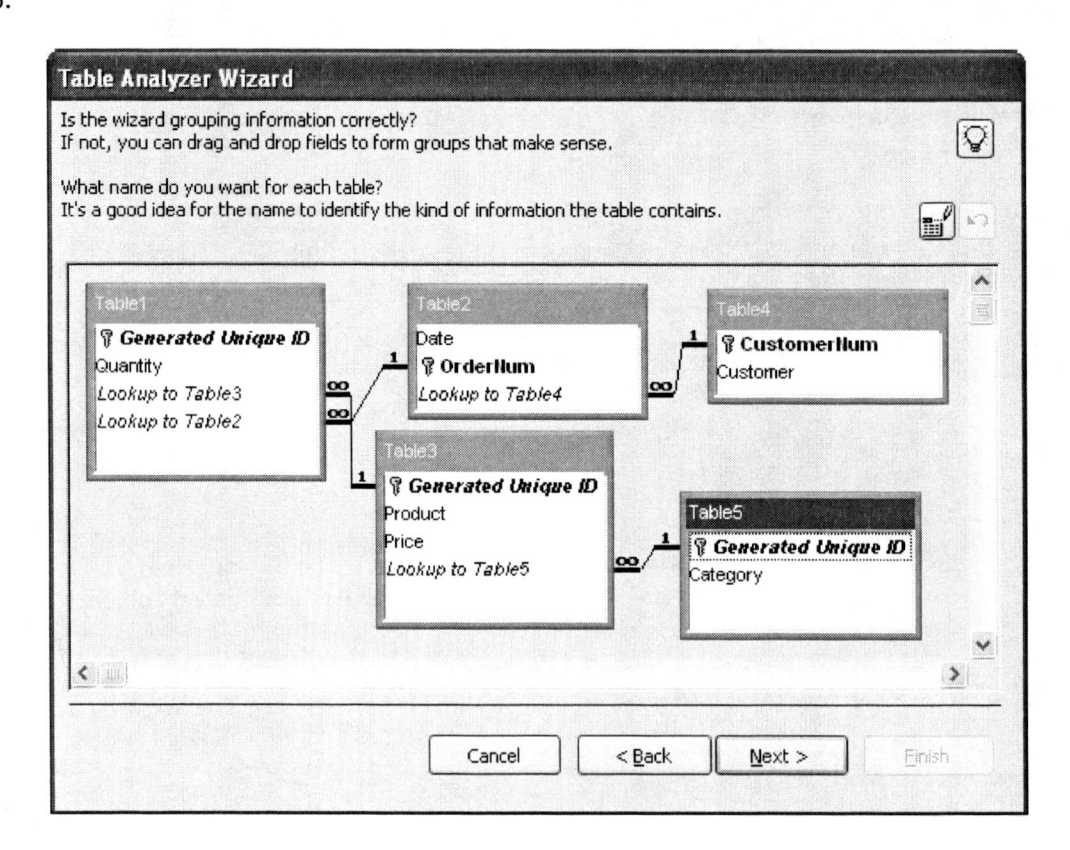

**Do you agree with the way the wizard has grouped the data into tables?**

_____

_____

7. In the Table Analyzer Wizard, rename the tables as follows:
   - Table1 to tblOrderDetails
   - Table2 to tblOrders
   - Table3 to tblProducts
   - Table4 to tblCustomers
   - Table5 to tblCategories

   **Continue with the wizard.**

   In this course, an Access object naming convention is used.

   a. **Select Table1.**

   b. **Click the Rename Table button.**

   c. **Type *tblOrderDetails***

   d. **Click OK.**

   e. **Rename the remaining tables as follows:**
      - Table2 to tblOrders
      - Table3 to tblProducts
      - Table4 to tblCustomers
      - Table5 to tblCategories

   f. **Click Next.**

# LESSON 1

8. **Do you agree with the primary key fields identified by the wizard? If necessary, refer to the original data.**

---

9. **Complete the wizard. When prompted to make corrections, leave all data as is. Do not create a query to generate a datasheet that looks like the original table. Save and close the database.**

    a. **Click Next.**

    b. **From the Correction column drop-down list, select (Leave As Is) for all entries.**

    | Product | Price | Correction |
    |---|---|---|
    | Bivy tent | $199.00 | |
    | Day pack | $65.00 | (Leave as is) |
    | Double bag | $99.99 | Cabin tent  $259 |
    | Down bag | $109.99 | Camp bag  $59.' |
    | Expedition pack | $49.50 | Camp kitchen  $59.' |
    | Fanny pack | $25.00 | Cooler  $29.' |
    | Mummy bag | $89.00 | Dome tent  $129 |
    | Rucksack | $49.50 | Duffel bag  $24.' |
    | | | Lantern  $39.' |

    c. **Click Next.**

    d. **Select No, Don't Create The Query.**

    e. **Uncheck the Display Help On Working With The New Tables Or Query? option.**

    f. **Click Finish.**

    g. **Click OK.**

---

10. **Have the data problems been eliminated?**

---

11. **Is there anything in the design of some of the tables that you are not used to seeing in your own tables?**

---

12. **Save and close the database.**

    a. **Save and close the database.**

---

*Lesson 1: Structuring Existing Data*

# LESSON 1

# TOPIC C

# Create a Junction Table

Even after running the Table Analyzer Wizard, your data may be redundant and difficult to read. One way you can alleviate some of the redundancy in your tables is by using a junction table. In this topic, you will create a *junction table*.

Suppose you have two tables that already have a relationship, but contain a great deal of redundant data. The redundant data can make the tables very difficult to understand and substantially slow down database performance. The creation of a junction table can clear up your tables, and allow your database to run much faster.

## Many-to-Many Relationships

**Definition:**

A *many-to-many relationship* is an association between two Access tables where multiple records in one table can correspond to multiple records in the other table. The number of records that correspond can vary, but there must be at least two in each table.

**Example:**

An example of two tables with a many-to-many relationship would be tables containing data about orders and products. Each order could include many products and each product could be included on many orders.

## Junction Tables

**Definition:**

A junction table is a table that eliminates a many-to-many relationship between two other tables. The junction table's *primary key* will consist of both the foreign keys from the other tables, thereby eliminating the duplicate records. The number of fields included in the junction table may vary.

**Example:**

When there are two tables that have a many-to-many relationship, a junction table can be used to eliminate the duplicate records. Figure 1-2 illustrates how a junction table might be used.

**Figure 1-2:** *The junction table eliminates the many-to-many relationship.*

## How to Create a Junction Table

**Procedure Reference: Create a Junction Table and Add Existing Data**

To create a junction table and add existing data:

1. Create a new table containing the fields that are the primary keys of the tables with the many-to-many relationship.
2. Designate the combination of those fields as the primary key of the junction table.
3. Name and save the table.
4. Create a query based on the original table that contains the fields in the junction table.
5. Change the query type to an Append query.
6. In the Table Name box, select the Junction table.
7. Verify that the Append To row indicates the appropriate fields in the destination table.
8. Run the query and confirm the addition of the records.
9. If a message is displayed that not all records can be appended, click Yes to ignore the errors and run the query.

# ACTIVITY 1-3

## Creating the Junction Table and Adding Data

### Data Files:

- JunctionTable.mdb

### Scenario:

One of the Human Resources staff has come to you for help. She was asked to keep track of what employees are working on what internal projects and tried to create an Access database to do that. She realizes that there's something wrong with the design of the tables because, when she went to create the table relationships, Access couldn't determine the relationship type.

# LESSON 1

| What You Do | How You Do It |
|---|---|
| 1. In JunctionTable.mdb, **create a table** with the fields *EmployeeID* (Text and a Field Size of 4) and *ProjectNum* (Text and a Field Size of 5). Make both fields the primary key of the table and name the table *tblAssignments*.<br><br>Close the table's Design view when done.<br><br>⚠ Make sure you enter the field sizes correctly or you could lose data when you run the query to add the data. | a. In JunctionTable.mdb, **create a table** in Design view.<br><br>b. Enter the Field Name *EmployeeID* with a Text Data Type and a Field Size of *4*<br><br>c. Enter the field *ProjectNum* with a Text data type and a Field Size of *5*<br><br>d. Select the EmployeeID and ProjectNum fields.<br><br>e. **Click the Primary Key button.**<br><br>f. Save the table with the name *tblAssignments*<br><br>g. Close the table's Design view. |
| 2. Create a query that will add the EmployeeID and ProjectNum values from tblEmployees to the new tblAssignments. Run the query to the point where you are notified that Access cannot append all the records. | a. Create a new query in Design view.<br><br>b. Add tblEmployees to the query from the Show Table window. Close the Show Table window.<br><br>c. Add the EmployeeID and ProjectNum fields to the design grid.<br><br>d. Choose Query→Append Query.<br><br>e. In the Append dialog box, **click the Table Name drop-down arrow, select tblAssignments, and then click OK.**<br><br>f. **Click the Run button.**<br><br>g. In the message box, **click Yes.** |
| 3. Why can't Access append all the records? | |

4. Continue the query and, when done, close the query without saving changes to the design. Open tblAssignments to verify the transfer of the data and close the table when done.

   a. In the message box notifying you that Access can't append six records due to key violations, **click Yes**.

   b. **Close the query without saving the design.**

   c. **Open tblAssignments and review the data;** there should be 62 records.

   d. **Close tblAssignments.**

# TOPIC D
# Improve Table Structure

Over the course of time, the table structure of a database may need to be changed to meet the needs of the company at that moment. For example, a company might give you a new target design structure that could require you to restructure a table, or hide columns for printing. In this topic, you will improve the table structure to meet a target design.

Your boss gives you a database that needs to be updated to meet the company's target specifications. Attempting to make the changes without first fully understanding how to restructure the tables could lead to a lot of extra work.

## How to Improve Table Structure

### Procedure Reference: Restructure a Table

To restructure a table:

1. Copy the structure of the existing tables to new tables.
2. Delete any unnecessary fields in the new tables and set primary keys.
3. Create queries to move the required data to the new tables.
4. Delete the old tables.
5. Rename the new tables.
6. Set the relationships between the new tables.

### Procedure Reference: Hide a Table Column

To hide a table column:

1. Open the table in which you want to hide a column.
2. Right-click the column heading of the column you want to hide.
3. From the drop-down list, select Hide Columns.

# LESSON 1

# ACTIVITY 1-4

## Modifying the Original Tables and Completing the Design

### Setup:
JunctionTable.mdb is open.

### Scenario:
Now that you have created the junction table, tblAssignments, you need to change the original tables to comply with your design. There is a good chance that there could be some duplicate records, and the table relationships will need to be cleaned up and updated.

| What You Do | How You Do It |
|---|---|
| 1. Copy and paste the structure of tblEmployees as *TempEmployees*.<br><br>Do the same for tblProjects as *TempProjects*.<br><br>In both tables, **confirm that you did not paste the data.** | a. In the Database window, **select tblEmployees and click the Copy button.**<br><br>b. **Click Paste.**<br><br>c. In the Paste Table As dialog box, in the Table Name text box, **enter *TempEmployees***<br><br>d. In the Paste Options box, **select Structure Only.**<br><br>e. **Click OK.**<br><br>f. **Open TempEmployees to confirm that you did not paste the data. Close the datasheet.**<br><br>g. **Select tblProjects and create a new table with the same structure. Name the table *TempProjects*** |

Microsoft® Office Access 2003: Level 3

# Lesson 1

2. Delete the ProjectNum field from TempEmployees and set the EmployeeID field as the primary key. For TempProjects, delete the EmployeeID field and set ProjectNum as the primary key.

    a. Open TempEmployees in Design view.

    b. Delete the ProjectNum field.

    c. Click Yes at the window that appears.

    d. Set the EmployeeID field as the primary key.

    e. Save and close the table design.

    f. Open TempProjects in Design view.

    g. Delete the EmployeeID field.

    h. Set the ProjectNum field as the primary key.

    i. Save and close the table design.

# Lesson 1

3. Create and run a query that appends the data in the appropriate fields from tblEmployees to TempEmployees. Don't save the query design. Confirm that the data was added correctly. There should be 47 records in TempEmployees.

   a. **Create a new query in Design view.**

   b. **Add tblEmployees to the query.**

   c. **Close the Show Table window.**

   d. **Add the EmployeeID, EmployeeLastName, and EmployeeFirstName** fields to the design grid.

   e. **Choose Query→Append Query.**

   f. From the TableName drop-down list, **select TempEmployees and click OK.**

   g. **Click the Run button.**

   h. **Click Yes to append the rows.**

   i. **Click Yes** to ignore the errors and run the query.

   j. **Close the Query Design window without saving the design.**

   k. **Open TempEmployees and confirm that there are 47 unique records. Close the datasheet.**

4. Create another query to append the data in the appropriate fields from tblProjects to TempProjects. Confirm that the data was added correctly. There should be 10 unique records in TempProjects.

   a. Create a new query in Design view.

   b. Add tblProjects to the query.

   c. Close the Show Table window.

   d. Add the ProjectNum and ProjectName fields to the design grid.

   e. Choose Query→Append Query.

   f. From the TableName drop-down list, select TempProjects and click OK.

   g. Click the Run button.

   h. Click Yes to append the rows.

   i. Click Yes to ignore the errors and run the query.

   j. Close the Query Design window without saving the design.

   k. Open TempProjects and confirm that there are 10 records. Close the datasheet.

5. Delete tblEmployees and tblProjects from the database. Rename TempEmployees to *tblEmployees* and TempProjects to *tblProjects*.

   a. In the Database window, select tblEmployees and press Delete. Confirm the deletion and have Access delete its relationship to other tables.

   b. In the Database window, select tblProjects and press Delete. Confirm the deletion and empty the Access clipboard.

   c. Right-click TempEmployees and choose Rename.

   d. Type *tblEmployees*

   e. Rename TempProjects to *tblProjects*

*Lesson 1: Structuring Existing Data*

# LESSON 1

6. Open the Relationships window and add the three tables. Set a one-to-many relationship between tblEmployees and tblAssignments and enforce referential integrity in the relationship. Set a one-to-many relationship between tblProjects and tblAssignments and enforce referential integrity. Save the changes to the Relationships window.

    *When creating one-to-many relationships, drag the fields from the one side to the many side.*

    a. Click the Relationships button.

    b. From the Show Table window, **add tblAssignments and close the Show Table window.**

    c. **From tblEmployees, drag the EmployeeID field to the EmployeeID field in tblAssignments.**

    d. In the Edit Relationships dialog box, **check Enforce Referential Integrity and click Create.**

    e. **Create a relationship between ProjectNum in tblProjects and ProjectNum in tblAssignments, enforcing referential integrity.**

    f. **Close the Relationships window, saving the changes to the layout.**

7. Hide the EmployeeFirstName column in tblEmployees and print the table. Save and close the database when finished.

    a. **Open tblEmployees.**

    b. **Right-click the EmployeeFirstName column heading.**

    c. From the drop-down list, **select Hide Columns.**

    d. **Print the table.**

    e. **Save and close the database.**

## Lesson 1 Follow-up

In this lesson, you structured existing data. Effectively restructuring existing data will save you time with both troubleshooting and data entry.

1. Do you think the Table Analyzer Wizard will be helpful on the job?

2. What types of data do you think you might have to import in to Access?

# LESSON 2
# Writing Advanced Queries

**Lesson Time**
1 hour(s), 30 minutes

## Lesson Objectives:

In this lesson, you will use a variety of techniques to summarize and present data with queries. You will:

- Create queries that return records with unmatched values and records with duplicate values.
- Use criteria in a totals query to control how records are selected and summarized.
- Create a crosstab query to display data in summary form.
- Create a PivotTable and a PivotChart to effectively summarize query data.
- Create a PivotChart on a form.

# LESSON 2

## Introduction

You've used groups and totals in queries before to roll up your data so it has more meaning. You've also used calculated fields to do aggregate calculations like sums and averages. In this lesson, you'll see some additional techniques that you can use to convert large amounts of data into meaningful information and to get the exact records you want when using a query to group and total data.

Since databases often contain thousands of records, the ability to summarize the data in effective ways is an important skill. The way you use criteria will give you different results. Knowing other techniques for summarizing data will enable you to make the best presentation.

# TOPIC A

# Create Unmatched and Duplicates Queries

Previously, you have created queries to help you narrow the scope of your data. One particular way you might want to narrow your data is by looking for unmatched or duplicate records in a table. In this topic, you will create queries to search for unmatched and duplicate records in a table.

As the administrator of a database, one of your jobs will be to keep the database working as efficiently as possible. A major cause of database slowdown is erroneous or duplicate data in a table. You can keep these problems to a minimum by running queries to search out the errant data.

## How to Create Unmatched and Duplicates Queries

### Procedure Reference: Create an Unmatched Query

To create an *Unmatched query*:

1. From the Queries tab, click New.
2. Double-click Find Unmatched Query Wizard.
3. Select the table or query you want to search for unmatched records. Click Next.
4. Select the table or query you want to compare against your first selection. Click Next.
5. Match the corresponding fields between the two tables. Click Next.
6. Select the fields you want shown in the query results. Click Next.
7. Name the query and click Finish to complete.

### Procedure Reference: Create a Duplicates Query

To create a *Duplicates query*:

1. From the Queries tab, click New.

# Lesson 2

2. Double-click Find Duplicates Query Wizard.
3. Select the table or query you want to search for duplicate records. Click Next.
4. Select the fields that might contain duplicate entries. Click Next.
5. Select any additional fields you want to show in the query results. Click Next.
6. Name the query and click Finish to complete.

# ACTIVITY 2-1

## Creating Queries to Search for Unmatched and Duplicate Records

### Data Files:

- Contacts.mdb

### Scenario:

Up to this point, each member of the sales team has kept a separate contact list in Access for all their clients. Moving forward, the management would like to compile one complete list for all sales contacts. Since the sales force is not extremely well-versed in Access, you know there might be a few problems you run into before combining the lists. Before you combine the tables, you want to make sure there are no duplicate records, and you also want to check the individual tables for duplicates.

| What You Do | How You Do It |
| --- | --- |
| 1. With Contacts.mdb open, start a new Find Unmatched Query Wizard. | a. Open Contacts.mdb.<br><br>b. From the Queries tab, **click New**.<br><br>c. From the New Query list, **double-click Find Unmatched Query Wizard**. |

*Lesson 2: Writing Advanced Queries*

# Lesson 2

2. **Complete the wizard comparing Susan's contacts against John's. Use the company names as matching fields. The query result needs to show only the company names. Close the query when finished.**

   a. From the list on the first screen of the wizard, **select Table: Susan's Contacts and click Next.**

   b. On the second screen of the wizard, **verify that Table: John's Contacts is highlighted and click Next.**

   c. **Highlight Company Name under both Susan's Contacts and John's Contacts. Click the <=> button** to match the fields.

   d. **Click Next.**

   e. From the Available Fields list, **highlight Company Name. Click the right arrow to move it to the Selected Fields list. Click Next.**

   f. **Accept the default name for the query and click Finish to complete the wizard.**

   g. The query now lists the nine company names that appear in Susan's contacts, but not John's. **Close the Query window when complete.**

3. **Start a new Find Duplicates Query Wizard.**

   a. From the Queries tab, **click New.**

   b. From the New Query list, **double-click Find Duplicates Query Wizard.**

---

22  Microsoft® Office Access 2003: Level 3

4. Check Susan's contacts for duplicate records by comparing company names. The company names are the only field the query needs to return. Save and close the database when finished.

   a. From the list on the first screen of the wizard, **select Table: Susan's Contacts and click Next.**

   b. From the Available Fields list, **select Company Name and move it to the Duplicate-Value Fields list. Click Next.**

   c. Since you don't need any fields other than the Company Name, **click Next** to advance the wizard.

   d. **Accept the default name for the query and click Finish to complete the wizard.**

   e. The query now shows the three duplicate records in Susan's contacts and how many times they are repeated.

   f. **Save and close the database when complete.**

# TOPIC B

# Group and Summarize Records Using the Criteria Field

You've probably used Totals queries frequently to arrive at aggregate data for groups of records in your database. In this topic, you'll see how using the Criteria field in different ways affects the set of records returned by your Totals queries.

Imagine that you are working with a 100,000 record database, but you only need to find a very small subset of those records that match a specific ID number. Using the Criteria field can take what would be a very tedious task, and make it happen in just a few seconds.

## The Criteria Field

The *Criteria field* allows you to apply conditions to your queries. You can limit the records returned by a query to only those that meet specific requirements that you declare.

# LESSON 2

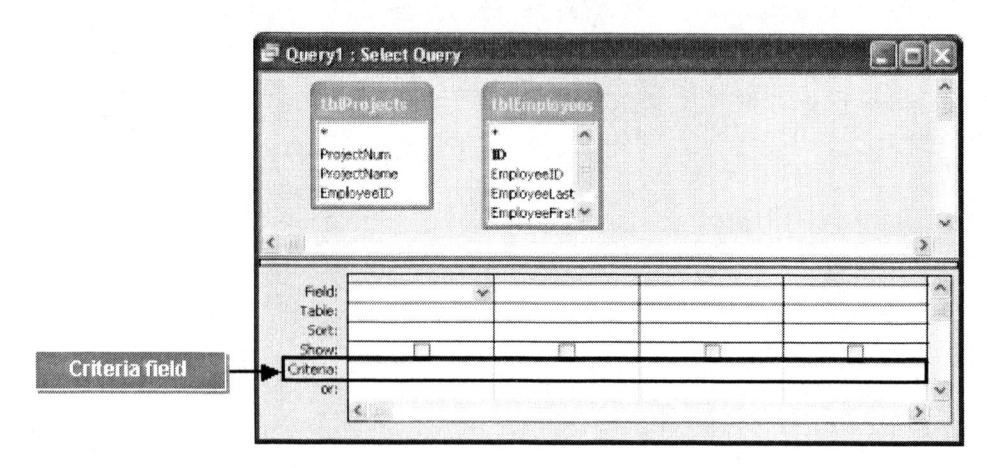

**Figure 2-1:** *The Criteria field.*

## How to Group and Summarize Records using the Criteria Field

### Procedure Reference: Summarize Data Using the Criteria Field

To summarize data using the Criteria field:

1. Open an existing query in Design view.
2. From the field that you wish to sort on, enter the qualifications in the Criteria field.
3. Run the query and examine the new results.

# ACTIVITY 2-2

## Summarizing Records in Different Ways with Criteria

### Data Files:

- Summarize.mdb

### Scenario:

You've been asked to provide some data about the purchasing volume of your customers. You want to see how many of your products each customer has bought and then home in on the largest volumes. You've been asked to:

- Look at the total amount of each product purchased by each customer.
- Create a list of customers and products where the total purchases were greater than $5,000.
- From the list of customers and products greater than $5,000, list only the records dated March 1st 2001 or later.

# Lesson 2

| What You Do | How You Do It |
|---|---|
| 1. In Summarize.mdb, **open the query qtotCustomerTotals and note the total number of records.** Switch to Design view. | a. Open Summarize.mdb. <br><br> b. From the Queries tab, **double-click qtotCustomerTotals.** <br><br> c. Verify that there are 70 records and switch to Design view. |

*There are 70 records in the datasheet resulting from the original query.*

2. What are the groupings of records?

3. Increase the TotalSales column width so you can view the entire expression.

   a. Drag the right side of the TotalSales column out so you can view the entire expression.

   *The formula field in the totals query looks complex, but when a totals query is first created, the user does not have to use the sum function in the field formula. A formula that multiplies Quantity by Price is first created, with the Total row set to SUM. After the query is saved, Access changes the design grid contents to use the Sum function. This query also uses a CCur function to convert the answer to currency. An alternative to the CCur function, simplifying the formula construction, would be to format the field output to currency using the query field properties.*

4.

TotalSales: Sum(CCur([tblOrderDetails!Quantity]*[tblProducts!Price]))

What is the purpose of the calculated expression?

*Lesson 2: Writing Advanced Queries*

# Lesson 2

5. You first want to see how many products had sales greater than $5,000. **Enter the criteria to view the products that had sales greater than $5,000. Run the query and note the new total number of records.**

   *There are 35 records in the datasheet. Only those products with total sales greater than $5,000 and the customers who made those purchases are displayed.*

   a. In the Criteria row for the TotalSales field, **type >5000**

   b. **Run the query.**

   c. **Verify that there are now only 35 records showing. Switch to Design view.**

6. **Enter the criteria to view records dated 3/1/01 or later. Run the query and note the new total number of records. Close the query without saving the changes.**

   a. From the tblOrders field list, **drag the Date field to the first open column.**

   b. In the Total field of the Date column, **select Where from the drop-down list.**

   c. In the Criteria field of the Date column, **type >3/1/01**

   d. **Run the query and verify that there are 15 matching records.**

   e. **Close the datasheet without saving changes to the design.**

# Topic C

## Summarize Data with a Crosstab Query

You know how valuable a totals query can be in summarizing data. Another type of query, a *crosstab query*, enables you to summarize values in a slightly different way. This topic will show you how.

As different areas of a business use a database, they will all have specific needs for how that data is displayed. Being able to summarize table data in multiple different ways makes this a much easier task. One method of data summarization is using a crosstab query. In this topic, you will summarize data using a crosstab query.

## Crosstab Query

**Definition:**

A crosstab query is a query that calculates and summarizes table data. Using the Crosstab Query Wizard, the user can choose what data will be displayed for the row and column headings, and how the intersecting data is calculated. The data can be calculated as a sum, average, or one of several other operations.

**Example:**

Figure 2-2 illustrates a crosstab query being created in the wizard.

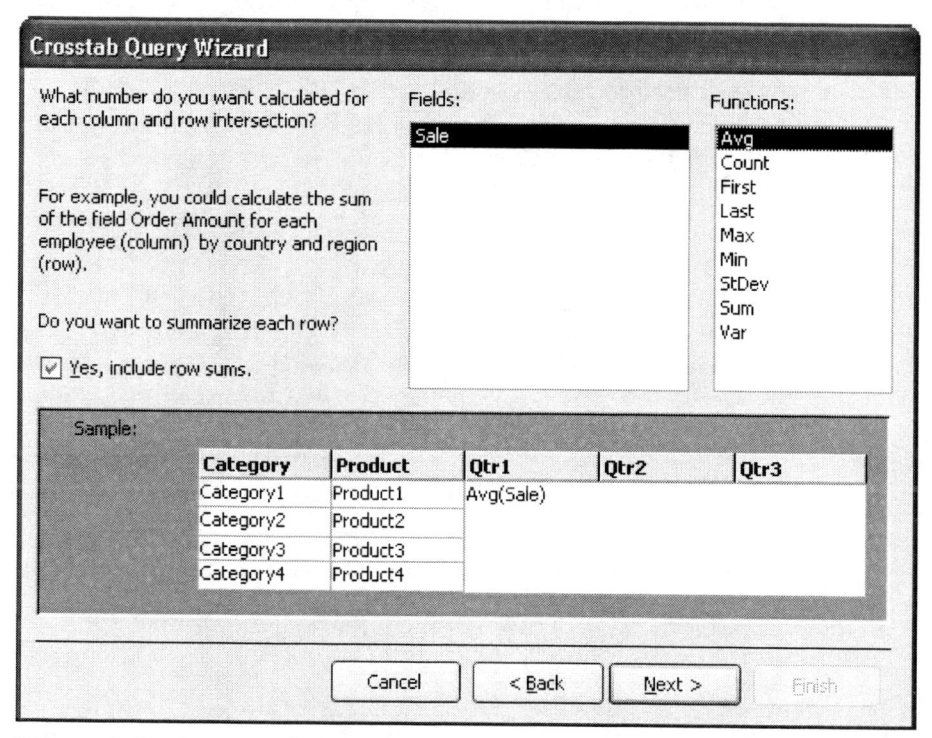

**Figure 2-2:** *A crosstab query being created in the wizard.*

*Lesson 2: Writing Advanced Queries*

# LESSON 2

## How to Summarize Data with a Crosstab Query

### Procedure Reference: Summarize Data with a Crosstab Query

To summarize data with a crosstab query:

1. In the Database window, display the query objects.
2. On the Database window toolbar, click New.
3. In the New Query dialog box, select Crosstab Query Wizard, and then click OK.
4. Specify the fields whose values will be the row and column headings.
5. Specify the field containing the data you want summarized according to the values in the rows and columns and the summary operation to be performed.
6. Select whether to run the query or see the query's structure in Design view and click Finish.

# ACTIVITY 2-3

## Summarizing Data with a Crosstab Query

### Setup:
Summarize.mdb is open.

### Scenario:
The sales manager wants to know how each product in each category did in the way of sales in each month of the first quarter. You've created a select query, qselQ1Sales, to extract the records you need and now you need to figure out how to summarize them to answer the sales manager's question. You've heard about crosstab queries and have decided to try out the Crosstab Query Wizard to see if that will yield the data you need. Once you get the right data, you'll refine the query design to get the display you want.

| What You Do | How You Do It |
| --- | --- |
| 1. Familiarize yourself with the design of the query, qselQ1Sales. Then, run the query and examine the records. Close the datasheet when done. | a. **Open the query, qselQ1Sales, in Design view.** The query selects, from several tables, the Category, Product, and Date fields with the criteria that the sales date is in the first quarter. It also calculates the amount of each sale. |
| | b. **Run the query.** The datasheet contains 730 records—too much detail to answer the business question. |
| | c. **Close the datasheet.** |

# LESSON 2

2. Start the Crosstab Query Wizard and base the new query on qselQ1Sales.

   a. In the Database window on the Queries tab, click **New**.

   b. In the New Query dialog box, **select Crosstab Query Wizard and click OK.**

   c. In the View box, **select Queries.**

   d. In the list of queries, **select Query: qselQ1Sales.**

   e. **Click Next.**

3. Designate, in order, the values in the Category and Product fields as row headings. Then, select the values in the Date field to be column headings and group that information by Month. Select Sum as the calculation to be performed. Accept the assigned name for the query and view the results.

   a. In the Available Fields list, if necessary, **select Category and click the right-pointing arrow** to add the field to the Selected Fields list.

   b. In the Available Fields list, if necessary, **select Product and click the right-pointing arrow.**

   c. **Click Next.**

   d. Verify that Date is selected in the Field list and **click Next.**

   e. In the list of date groupings, **select Month and click Next.**

   f. Verify that Sale is selected in the Fields list and **select Sum in the Functions list.**

   g. **Click Next.**

   h. **Click Finish.**

4. What are the features of the resulting datasheet?

5. Switch to Design view.

   a. Switch to Design view.

*Lesson 2: Writing Advanced Queries*

29

# Lesson 2

6. **What features do you notice in the design created by the wizard?**

___

7. **Change the appropriate query property so that the extra columns for the other months are not displayed. Run the query. Move the Total Of Sale column to the right of the Mar column, save the design changes, and close the datasheet.**

   a. In the open space on the top half of the query, **right-click and choose Properties.**

   b. In the Query Properties sheet, **right-click the Column Headings property box and choose Zoom.**

   c. **Delete everything after the closing double-quotes for the month of Mar and click OK.**

   d. **Close the Properties window.**

   e. **Run the query.**

   f. **Select the Total Of Sale column and drag it to the right of the Mar column.**

   g. **Save the query.**

   h. **Close the datasheet.**

# ACTIVITY 2-4

## Understanding How to Summarize Data with a Crosstab Query

**Scenario:**
Your manager has been pleased with some of the data you have been providing from queries that perform aggregate functions to summarize data. However, she has now asked that you summarize the data a bit differently, and the techniques you have used thus far will not accomplish the goal. It is time to review your understanding of how to summarize data with a crosstab query.

| What You Do | How You Do It |
|---|---|

1. **What is the name of the wizard you can use to create a crosstab query?**

    a) Crosstab Wizard

    b) Crosstab Query Wizard

    c) Crosstab Filter Query Wizard

    d) Crosstab Filter Wizard

2. **Which of the following are true of creating crosstab queries with the Crosstab Query Wizard?**

    a) The result is a query that sorts data.

    b) The calculation used must be based on numeric data, and not on date datatypes.

    c) You can choose what data will be displayed for the row and column headings and how the intersecting data will be calculated.

    d) The data calculation can only be a sum or an average.

*Lesson 2: Writing Advanced Queries*

LESSON 2

# TOPIC D

# Create a PivotTable and a PivotChart

You've seen how a crosstab query can be a powerful tool for summarizing data. You can easily print the datasheet or create a report on the data. In this topic, you'll see how to create objects that summarize data in much the same way as a crosstab query, but in a format the Access user can interact with to see the data in different ways.

Often, someone will ask you for summary data and, as soon as you give it to them, they say "Now could I see it this other way?" Interactive *PivotTables* and *PivotCharts* enable the Access user to manipulate the summary data and therefore may save you from having to create multiple queries and reports for them.

## PivotTable

### Definition:

A PivotTable is a database view that allows you to summarize and examine data in a datasheet or form. A PivotTable is created by dragging the desired fields to the appropriate area on the design screen. Data can also be broken down to different levels of detail, such as showing earnings by year, quarter, or month.

### Example:

Figure 2-3 illustrates the design view of a PivotTable.

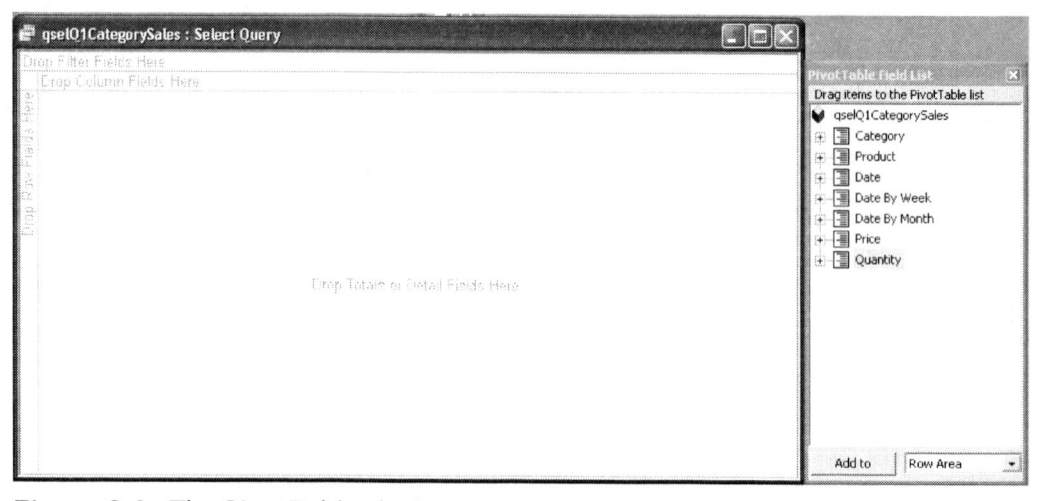

**Figure 2-3:** *The PivotTable design view screen.*

## PivotChart

### Definition:

A PivotChart is a database view that shows a graphical analysis of data in a datasheet or form. A PivotChart is created by dragging the desired fields to the appropriate area on the design screen. Data can be broken down to different levels of detail and unwanted items can be hidden from view.

Microsoft® Office Access 2003: Level 3

# Lesson 2

### Example:

Figure 2-4 illustrates the design view of a PivotChart.

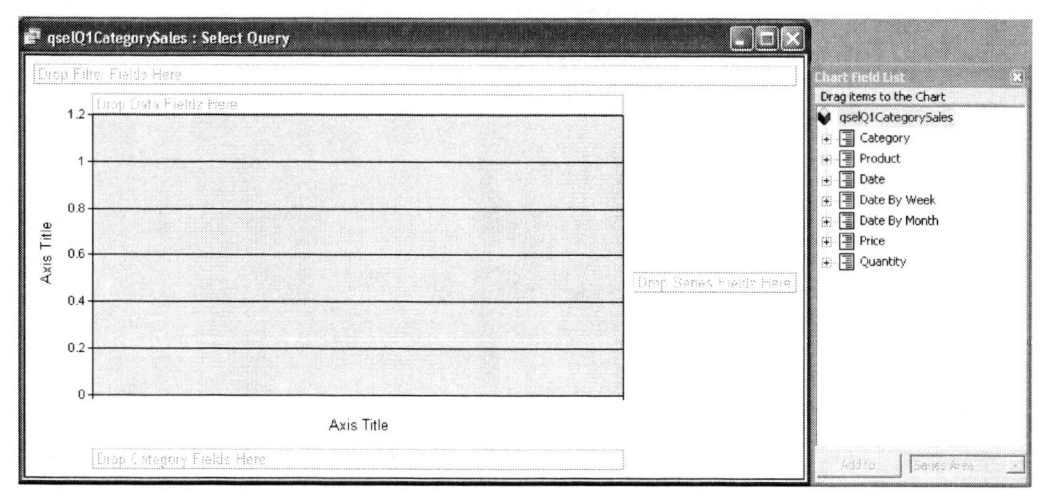

**Figure 2-4:** *The PivotChart design view screen.*

## How to Create a PivotTable and a PivotChart

### Procedure Reference: Create a PivotTable View

To create a PivotTable view:

1. Open the query.
2. Choose View→PivotTable View.
3. Add the Filter, Row, and Column fields.
4. Add the field or fields to be included in the Detail Data area.
5. Add any calculated totals or fields.
6. Modify the view to suit your information needs.

### Procedure Reference: Create a PivotChart View

To create a PivotChart view:

1. Choose View→PivotChart View.
2. Modify the chart layout.
3. Modify the chart type to suit your needs.
4. Save the query.

*Lesson 2: Writing Advanced Queries*

# LESSON 2

# ACTIVITY 2-5

## Creating a PivotTable View

**Setup:**
Summarize.mdb is open.

**Scenario:**
It seems like the Vice President of Sales is never satisfied. As soon as you give her the summary data she asks for, she wants to see the same data summarized in a slightly different way. You would like to provide her the data in a way that she can manipulate herself.

| What You Do | How You Do It |
|---|---|
| 1. Open the qselQ1CategorySales query and create a PivotTable view with the following parameters:<br>• The Category field as a Filter.<br>• The Product field as Rows.<br>• The Date By Month field as Columns.<br>• The Price and Quantity fields as Detail Data. | a. Open the qselQ1CategorySales query and choose View→PivotTable View.<br><br>b. In the PivotTable Field List window, select the Category field and drag it to the PivotTable design window over the words Drop Filter Fields Here.<br><br>c. Drag the Product field to the Drop Row Fields Here area.<br><br>d. Drag the Date By Month field to the Drop Column Fields Here area.<br><br>e. Drag both the Price and Quantity fields to the Drop Totals or Detail Fields Here area.<br><br>f. Close the PivotTable Field List window. |

# LESSON 2

2. **Create a calculated detail field that multiplies the Price and Quantity fields. Give it a Caption of *Sale* and set its Number format to Currency.**

   a. From the menu bar, **choose PivotTable→Calculated Totals And Fields→Create Calculated Detail Field.**

   b. In the text area below the Name text box, **select the 0 and type *Price*Quantity***

      **Click Change.**

   c. In the Properties dialog box, **select the Captions tab.**

   d. **Select the entry in the Caption text box, type *Sale* and press Enter.**

   e. **Select the Format tab.**

   f. From the Number drop-down list, **select Currency.**

   g. **Close the Properties dialog box.**

3. **Designate the Sale field as a Sum calculation and then hide details in the PivotTable view.**

   a. **Select the Sale field in the PivotTable view by clicking its column heading.**

   b. **Click the AutoCalc button and select Sum.**

   c. **Click the Hide Details button.**

*Lesson 2: Writing Advanced Queries* 35

# LESSON 2

4. Expand the view of 2001 and Qtr1. Remove the Years and Quarters column heading labels from the PivotTable view.

   a. Click the expand indicator (+) next to 2001.

   b. Expand Qtr1.

   c. In the column heading area, **select the Years field button and drag it out of the window until an X appears.**

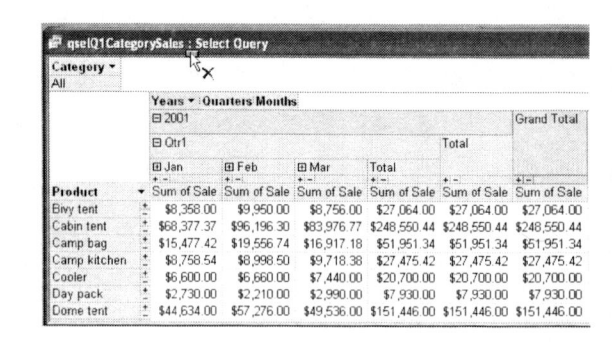

   d. In the column heading area, **select the Quarters field button and drag it out of the window until an X appears.**

5. Use the Category drop-down list to confine the view to the product category Tents. View the other categories. When done, display all of the categories, and then close the window, saving changes to the layout.

   a. Open the Category drop-down list and uncheck All.

   b. **Check Tents and click OK.**

   c. Use the Category drop-down list to view the data for other categories.

   d. When done, **display all categories.**

   e. **Close the PivotTable view window, saving changes to the layout.**

# ACTIVITY 2-6

## Working with a PivotChart

### Setup:
Summarize.mdb is open.

### Scenario:
You would like to give the Vice President of Sales as many options as possible for viewing the data and you know she responds well to a graphical representation.

| What You Do | How You Do It |
|---|---|
| 1. Open qselQ1CategorySales and verify the presence of the PivotTable view. Create a PivotChart view of the data and display the Legend. | a. Open qselQ1CategorySales.<br><br>b. Choose View→PivotTable View.<br><br>c. Choose View→PivotChart View.<br><br>d. On the PivotChart toolbar, click the Show Legend button.<br><br>e. Close the Chart Field List window. |
| 2. View the chart for the Tents category. Pivot the chart so the horizontal axis is for the months and the bars represent each product. Return to PivotTable view to view the data. | a. Using the Category drop-down list, view the chart for the Tents category.<br><br>b. Select the Months field button and drag it next to the Product label.<br><br>c. Select the Product field button and drag it to the Drop Series Fields Here area.<br><br>d. Choose View→PivotTable View. The changes made in the PivotChart have affected the appearance of the PivotTable. |

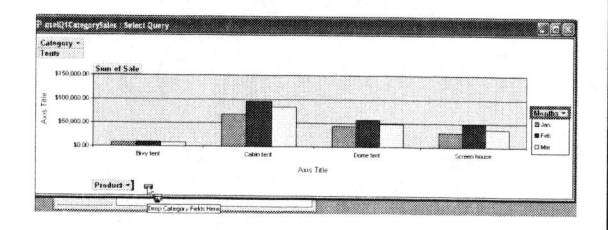

*Lesson 2: Writing Advanced Queries*

**LESSON 2**

37

# Lesson 2

3. Switch to PivotChart view and pivot the chart again so Months are the Series fields and Products are the Category fields. View the data as different types of column charts, finally ending with a 3-D column chart.

   a. Choose View→PivotChart View.

   b. Pivot the chart again so the Months are again the Series fields and Products are the Category fields.

   c. If necessary, to order the months correctly in the legend, **right-click the Months field button and choose Sort→ Sort Ascending.**

   d. **Right-click a gray area of the chart and choose Chart Type.**

   e. **Move the Properties dialog box so you can view its contents and the chart.**

   f. In the thumbnails of the Column charts, **select a different chart type and view the effect on the PivotChart.**

   g. After you have tried several different column charts, **select the 3D column chart.**

4. Add a vertical Axis Title of *Sales* and delete the horizontal Axis Title. Close the PivotChart window and save all changes when complete.

   a. From the Chart window, **click the vertical Axis Title.**

   b. On the Format tab of the Properties window, **select the Caption text box and type *Sales***

   c. Press Enter.

   d. Click the horizontal Axis Title and press Delete.

   e. Close the Properties dialog box.

   f. Close the PivotChart window, saving the changes to the layout.

*Microsoft® Office Access 2003: Level 3*

# TOPIC E

# Display a Graphical Summary on a Form

You have previously worked with PivotCharts as part of your queries, but that is not the only way they can be used. In this topic, you will create a PivotChart on a form, starting with the Form Wizard.

The PivotChart view of a query is available to the user only after he or she opens the query and changes to that view. The advantage to creating a PivotChart on a form is that it's immediately available when the *form* is opened.

## How to Display a Graphical Summary on a Form

### Procedure Reference: Create a PivotChart on a Form

To create a PivotChart on a form:

1. Create a new form using the Form Wizard.
2. Select the data source for the PivotChart.
3. Select the fields for the PivotChart.
4. In the list of layouts, select PivotChart.
5. Select a style.
6. Enter a title for the PivotChart.
7. In the PivotChart, drag the appropriate fields to the Category, Series, and Data Fields areas. Optionally, drag a field to the Filter Fields area.
8. Display a legend.
9. Make desired changes to the PivotChart display and axis titles.
10. Save and close the form.

# LESSON 2

# ACTIVITY 2-7

## Creating a PivotChart on a Form

**Setup:**
Summarize.mdb is open.

**Scenario:**
You think that a PivotChart is a very effective presentation of data. Your Customer Service people use a form you created, frmCustomersOrders, to check on customers' orders. It might be helpful if they could easily see the purchase volume of the customer over a certain number of months.

> 📌 The sample database used in this activity contains sales only for January, February, and March. The exact steps used in creating the legend on the PivotChart reflect that data.

| What You Do | How You Do It |
|---|---|
| 1. Using the Form Wizard, **base a new form on all the fields in the qselCustExtended query. Select a PivotChart layout and a style. Give the form the title *myPivotChartForm* and complete the wizard.**<br><br>📌 The form style is not relevant to a PivotChart layout and your selection of a style will not be reflected in the form. | a. From the Forms tab, **double-click Create Form By Using Wizard.**<br><br>b. **Base the form on the qselCustExtended query and add all fields to the form.**<br><br>c. **Click Next.**<br><br>d. In the list of layouts, **select PivotChart and click Next.**<br><br>e. **Select a style and click Next.**<br><br>f. **Enter a title of *myPivotChartForm* and click Finish.** |
| 2. In the PivotChart, **use CustomerName as the Category field, Date By Month as the Series field, and ExtendedPrice as the Data field. Close the Chart Field List window.**<br><br>📌 You may need to move the Chart Field List window to see the components of the PivotChart. | a. **Drag the CustomerName field to the Drop Category Fields Here area.**<br><br>b. **Drag the Date By Month field to the Drop Series Fields Here area.**<br><br>c. **Drag the ExtendedPrice field to the Drop Data Fields Here area.**<br><br>d. **Close the Chart Field List window.** |

# Lesson 2

3. Display a legend that shows the months of Jan, Feb, and Mar.

   a. Click the Show Legend button.

   b. Right-click the Years Field button and choose Expand.

   c. Right-click the Quarters Field button and choose Expand.

   d. Drag the Years and Quarters Field buttons off the form.

4. Change the vertical Axis Title to *Purchases* and delete the horizontal Axis Title. Save and close the form.

   a. Select the vertical Axis Title and click the Properties button.

   b. Change the entry in the Caption text box to *Purchases*

   c. Close the Properties dialog box.

   d. Select the horizontal Axis Title and press Delete.

   e. Save and close the form.

*Lesson 2: Writing Advanced Queries*

# Lesson 2

5. Open frmCustomerOrders in Design view and, using the Control Wizards, add a subform control to the form. Use myPivotChartForm as the subform and define a link between the two forms using the CustomerName field. Accept the default name for the form.

   a. Open frmCustomerOrders in Design view and maximize the window.

   b. In the Toolbox, **verify that Control Wizards is selected.**

   c. **Click the Subform/Subreport tool.**

   d. **Click in frmCustomerOrders to create a subform control.**

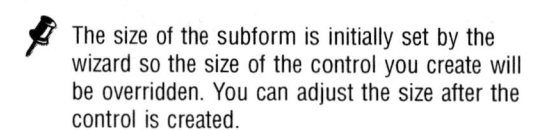

   > The size of the subform is initially set by the wizard so the size of the control you create will be overridden. You can adjust the size after the control is created.

   e. In the SubForm Wizard dialog box, **select Use An Existing Form.**

   f. **Select myPivotChartForm and click Next.**

   g. **Click Define My Own.**

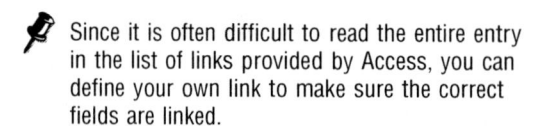

   > Since it is often difficult to read the entire entry in the list of links provided by Access, you can define your own link to make sure the correct fields are linked.

   h. **Click the Form/Report Fields drop-down arrow and select CustomerName.**

   i. **Click the Subform/Subreport Fields drop-down arrow and select CustomerName, and then click Next.**

   j. **Accept the default name for the subform and click Finish.**

# LESSON 2

6. Size the subform control to approximately 3 inches square. Then save the form as *myCustomerOrders* and view the form.

    a. Adjust the size of the subform control to approximately 3 inches square.

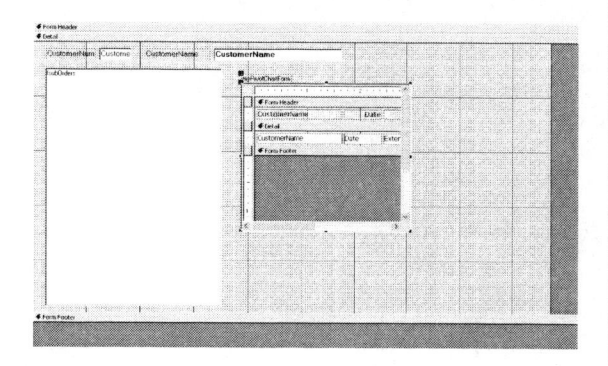

    b. Save the form as *myCustomerOrders*

    c. Change to Form view.

7. What data does the PivotChart show as you move through the records?

8. Save and close the database.

    a. Save and close the database.

# Lesson 2 Follow-up

In this lesson, you wrote advanced queries. Queries will help you to summarize your data in many different ways. Using every available summary technique will allow you to make the most effective presentation for your audience

1. How might you use Unmatched and Duplicates queries?

2. Will PivotCharts and PivotTables be useful on the job? Why?

*Lesson 2: Writing Advanced Queries*

# Notes

# LESSON 3
# Simplifying Tasks with Macros

**Lesson Time**
*45 minutes*

## Lesson Objectives:

In this lesson, you will create and revise basic Access macros.

You will:

- Create a macro that opens a form.
- Attach a macro to a command button.
- Add a Where condition expression to a macro.

# Lesson 3

## Introduction

You've explored ways to structure and summarize the data stored in your database. You're now ready to make it easier for database users to access that data by turning your attention toward database usability. In this lesson, you will learn how to create objects that simplify database activities.

Working with Access databases may require you to perform many repetitive actions. Using a *macro* can automate many of these tasks, saving you time and effort.

# Topic A

## Create a Macro

As you've probably noticed, building an Access database requires you to perform many repetitive actions. This can be very time consuming for you as the developer. Using macros will allow you to take those same tasks, and automate them. Creating macros takes a little extra time up front, but your efforts will pay off in the end.

Creating a macro is kind of like programming your car radio. Before you program in your favorite radio stations, you're stuck searching for the next good song by endlessly turning the tuning dial or scanning through each and every station. This can be tedious! So, you take a few minutes to program in all of the good stations, and finding fabulous tunes is as easy as pressing a button. It's the same way with creating macros. Once you take the time to create them, you'll soon be zipping around, saving time, and enjoying the muscle that macros add to your work in Access.

### Macros

**Definition:**

> A macro is an Access object that consists of a series of actions that are automatically performed for you. You can create a macro to automate a process or a series of tasks. Macros are stored as objects in the database and are listed under the Macros button in the Database window.

**Example:**

> Macros can be created for such tasks as opening a form for entering customer records; running a query and printing the results; finding and filtering records for a report; or importing data. You might create a macro to validate new data after it is entered by a user. Because a macro always runs the same way, it makes a process consistent.

### The Macro Window

Macros are created in the *Macro window*. The upper part of the window is where you add the actions that you want the macro to perform, such as opening a form. In the Action column, you can specify the action commands to be performed in the macro. Each macro can have one or more actions. In the Comments column, you can describe each action in the macro. Comments are optional, but they make it easier to understand and maintain the macro. The following figure illustrates the macro window.

# LESSON 3

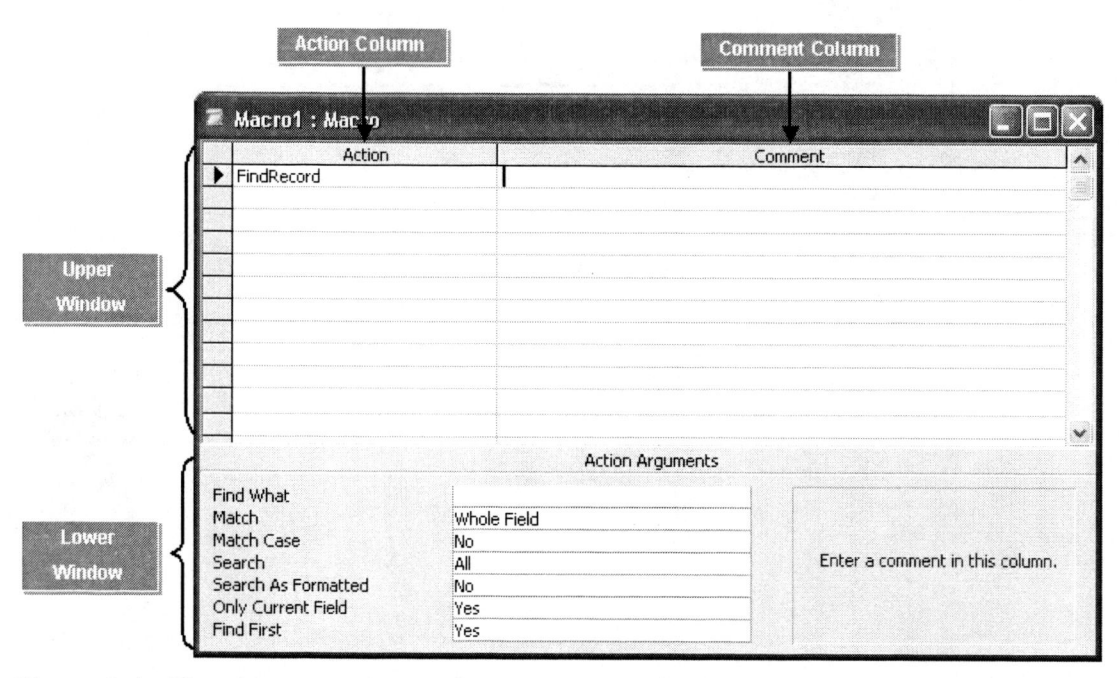

**Figure 3-1:** *The macro window.*

The lower part of the window is where you can specify arguments for an action. Arguments provide additional information to macro actions on how to carry out an action. For example, arguments can indicate what object or data to use. The arguments that are listed depend on the action you have chosen.

## How to Create a Macro

### Procedure Reference: Create a Macro

To create a macro:

1. In the Database window, display the macro objects.
2. Click New to open the Macro window.
3. Select the macro actions that you want the macro to perform.
4. For each action, define the action arguments.
5. Save the macro.
6. Test the macro.

Lesson 3: Simplifying Tasks with Macros

# LESSON 3

# ACTIVITY 3-1

## Creating a Macro to Open a Form

**Data Files:**

- Macro.mdb

**Scenario:**

The manager of the Sales department has come to you for help with the department's Access database. Currently, most customer data is accessed through one form, but the customer contact name is accessed through another. Sales agents must search through the Contact form to find the name of their contact at each customer's company. Sales agents could save time and be more efficient in setting up their calls if they could access the customer Contact form from the corresponding CustomerData form.

| What You Do | How You Do It |
|---|---|
| 1. Using Macro.mdb, **open a new Macro window.** | a. Using Macro.mdb with Macros selected in the Objects pane of the Database window, **click New** so that a new Macro window is displayed. |
| 2. In the first row of the Action column, **select Echo. Set the Echo On property to No.** | a. From the drop-down list in the first row of the Action column, **select Echo.** |
|  | b. In the Action Arguments pane, located in the lower-left corner, **click in the Echo On box** to display the drop-down arrow. |

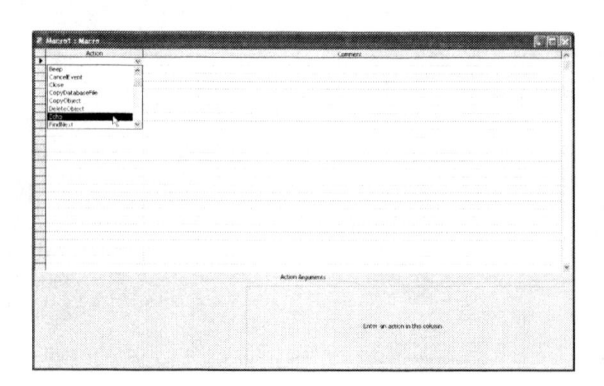

# LESSON 3

c. From the drop-down list, **select No.**

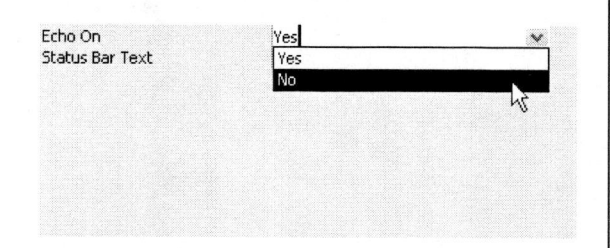

---

3. In the Action column's second row, **add the OpenForm action.**
   
   a. **Click the second row of the Action column.**
   
   b. From the drop-down list, **select OpenForm.**

---

4. In the Form Name property box, **select frmContact.**
   
   a. In the Action Arguments pane, **click the Form Name property box.**
   
   b. From the Form Name drop-down list, **select frmContact.**

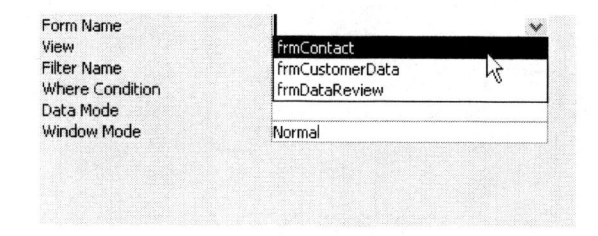

---

5. Save your macro as *mcrMyContact* and close the Macro window.
   
   a. **Click the Save button and name the macro *mcrMyContact***
   
   **Click OK.**
   
   b. **Close the Macro window.** 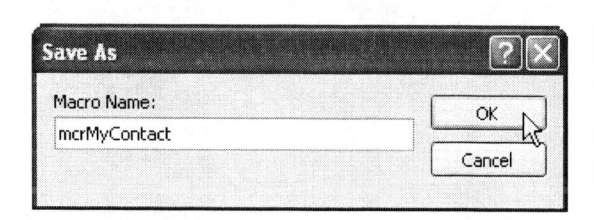

---

*Lesson 3: Simplifying Tasks with Macros*

# Lesson 3

6. **Run the mcrMyContact macro. Close the frmContact form.**

   a. In the Database window, **double-click the mcrMyContact macro.** The macro executes and displays the frmContact form.

   b. **Close the frmContact form.**

# Topic B
# Attach a Macro to a Command Button

You have just created your own macro. While the macro is saved in the database, it hasn't yet been added to a database application. The next step in putting your macro to work is to add it to a command button in an existing form.

Creating and saving a macro is a large part of the work involved in adding these powerful objects to your Access applications; however, if you leave the macro tucked away in your database file, it's doubtful that the folks who use your applications will ever stumble across this handy tool. One way to help users get the most out of the macros you create is to add them to command buttons in the appropriate database applications.

## Object Events

**Definition:**

An *object event* is an action that is caused by the user. An event can be anything that the user does to the database, such as clicking a button or opening a form. Object events can be used to trigger the macros you create.

**Example:**

An object event could be clicking a button, or resizing a form.

**Object Event Categories**

Forms, reports, and controls are the only objects in which Access recognizes events. These events can be categorized into several groups.

| Event Group | Examples |
| --- | --- |
| Window events | Open, close, or resize a window. |
| Data events | Update, delete, or make current. |
| Focus events | Activate, enter, or exit. |
| Keyboard events | Press or release a key. |
| Mouse events | Click or double-click the mouse button. |

| Event Group | Examples |
|---|---|
| Print events | Format and print. |
| Error and timing events | After an error or after some time has passed. |

## How to Attach a Macro to a Command Button

### Procedure Reference: Attach a Macro to a Command Button

To attach a macro to a command button:

1. In the Design view of a form, add a Command Button control.
2. Display the control properties.
3. Select the Event page.
4. Click in the box for the On Click property.
5. Use the drop-down list for the On Click property to select the macro you want to run when the command button is clicked.
6. Close the Properties sheet.
7. Save the form.
8. Test the command button.

# ACTIVITY 3-2

## Attaching a Macro to a Command Button

### Setup:
Macro.mdb is open.

### Scenario:
You have created the mcrMyContact macro that opens the frmContact form, just as the Sales Manager wished. Now, you need to add the macro functionality to a command button in the frmCustomerData form so that the Sales agents can take advantage of this time-saving feature.

| What You Do | How You Do It |
|---|---|
| 1. Open the frmCustomerData form in Design view. Deactivate the Control Wizards tool. | a. Open the frmCustomerData form in Design view. |
| | b. In the Toolbox, **click the Control Wizards button** to deactivate it. You will be creating a button from scratch. |

# Lesson 3

2. **Add a command button beneath the Fax label. Name the button *cmdContact* and change its caption to *Contact*.**

   a. **Click the Command Button tool.**

   b. In the Design view window, underneath the Fax label, **click to create a command button.**

   c. With the command button selected, **click the Properties button.**

   d. In the Name field on the All page with the existing text highlighted, **type *cmdContact***

   e. In the Caption field, **highlight the existing text and type *Contact***

3. Before attaching a macro to a control, you should determine when the macro will execute.

   **When do you want the macro to execute?**

4. **To what event should the macro be attached?**

5. **In the On Click property box, select mcrMyContact. Close the Properties sheet. Save the form as *frmMyCustomerData*.**

   a. From the cmdContact command button property window, **select the Event tab.**

   b. In the On Click property box, from the drop-down list, **select mcrMyContact.**

   c. **Close the Properties window.**

   d. **Save the form as *frmMyCustomerData***

52  Microsoft® Office Access 2003: Level 3

# Topic C

# Restrict Records Using a Where Condition

You've created a simple macro that opens a form. This functionality can be a real time saver. As you'll see in this topic, you can make your macro even more useful by refining it to select only certain records.

Simply adding a macro to a form doesn't always end in the desired result, as you've seen. If a macro is designed to open a form displaying customer contact information, but the information shown doesn't relate to the customer you need to call, it is of no use to you. Learning how to restrict records by using expressions and operators will allow you to tailor the results of your macro to better meet your users' needs.

## The Where Condition

**Definition:**

The *Where condition* is an argument that can be used to compare and restrict the records that are displayed on two related forms. Often, a Where condition is used to match values between fields in the form opened by the macro and those in the form containing the command button.

**Example:**

If you want to open a form and see only the records from the Marketing (MK) department, you should enter the following Where condition: [strDept]="MK"

The syntax is as follows:

[fieldname]=[Forms]![Formname]![controlname on other form]

## How to Restrict Records Using a Where Condition

**Procedure Reference: Restrict Records Using the Where Condition**

To restrict records using the Where condition:

1. On the Event page of the Properties sheet, click the Build button to open the Macro window.
2. Select the appropriate action.
3. In the Action Arguments pane, right-click the Where Condition box.
4. Select Zoom from the drop-down list and type the Where condition here.
5. Click OK.
6. Save the macro.
7. Close the Macro window and the Properties sheet.
8. Test the macro.

# LESSON 3

# ACTIVITY 3-3

## Entering an Expression in a Macro Argument

**Setup:**

Macro.mdb is open.

**Scenario:**

The macro you're working on for the Sales Manager doesn't work quite the way you had planned. When he used the macro to open the Contact form, the record displayed wasn't in sync with the record he was reviewing in the My CustomerData form. You know the new Where Condition in the macro should read

[CustomerNum]=[Forms]![frmMyCustomerData]![CustomerNum].

*(handwritten annotations: "child" under [CustomerNum], "parent" over [frmMyCustomerData]![CustomerNum])*

| What You Do | How You Do It |
|---|---|
| 1. In frmMyCustomerData, **display the Macro window for the On Click property of cmdContact.** | a. From the Design view of frmMyCustomerData, if necessary, **select the Contact button.** |
| | b. **Click the Properties button.** |
| | c. **Select the Event tab.** |
| | d. **Click in the On Click property box, and then click the Build button** [...]. The Macro window displays. |
| 2. **Activate the Zoom box to view the entire Where condition for the OpenForm action.** | a. In the Action column, **click the OpenForm entry.** |
| | b. In the Action Arguments pane, **right-click in the Where Condition box.** |
| | c. **Select Zoom** from the drop-down list. This will allow you to see the entire Where condition expression at one time. |

54    Microsoft® Office Access 2003: Level 3

# LESSON 3

3.  **Type the Where condition in the Zoom box. Save the Where condition.**

    a.  In the Zoom box, **type the code seen in the sample below.**

        *See Code Sample 1.*

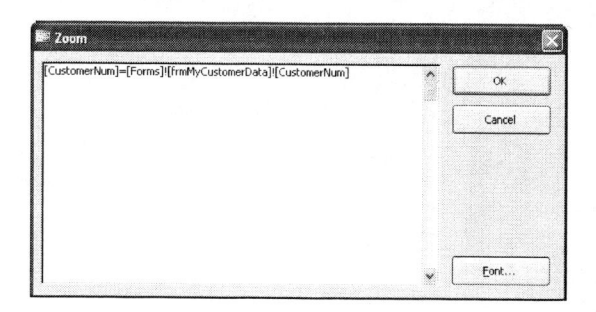

    b.  **Click OK.**

---

Code Sample 1

`[CustomerNum]=[Forms]![frmMyCustomerData]![CustomerNum]`

---

4.  **Save the macro. Close the Macro window, and then close the Properties sheet.**

    a.  **Click the Save button.**

    b.  On the Macro window, **click the Close button.**

    c.  In the Properties sheet, **click the Close button.**

---

5.  **Test the command button.**

    a.  **Click the Form View button.**

    b.  **Advance to record 2. Note the customer number for this record _____.**

    c.  **Click the Contact button.** The frmContact form opens. **Check the customer number against the one you noted from the frmCustomerData form.** The customer numbers should match.

    d.  **Save and close the form windows and database.**

---

*Lesson 3: Simplifying Tasks with Macros*

55

# LESSON 3

## Lesson 3 Follow-up

In this lesson, you simplified tasks using macros. Macros will allow you to automate many of the repetitive tasks you might have to perform when working with an Access database.

1. **Can you think of places where it might be helpful to attach a macro to a command button? Explain.**

2. **How might restricting records using a Where condition help you on the job?**

# LESSON 4

# Adding Interaction and Automation with Macros

**Lesson Time**
*50 minutes*

## Lesson Objectives:

In this lesson, you will create macros that improve data entry efficiency and integrity.

You will:

- Create a macro that makes data input a requirement.
- Create a macro that displays a message box.
- Create a macro that inputs data under certain conditions.

# Lesson 4

## Introduction

You now know how macros work and how to create one. As you've seen, macros can save time by easing access to your database contents. Next, you'll see how macros can add interaction and automation to your database applications. You can use macros to require data entry, send messages to database users, and even automate data entry.

Macros can do more than just automate simple tasks. For example, they can help to ensure the accuracy of the data being entered in your database by requiring data entry in certain fields and notifying the user of mistakes with message boxes.

# Topic A

## Require Data Entry with a Macro

Now that you know how to build a basic macro, you're ready to move on to creating more sophisticated macros. First, you'll create a macro that will prevent a record from being saved until certain required data has been entered.

If you're using your database application for data entry, you want to ensure the quality of the data being entered. Trying to ship ordered products to a company for which you have no address is frustrating and embarrassing. If you don't have a contact name noted, calling to sort things out can be even worse. Creating a macro to require data entry in certain fields will prompt users to complete vital information. This makes your records more accurate and useful.

### Macro Conditions

**Definition:**

> A *macro condition* is an expression that enables a macro to perform certain tasks only if a specific situation exists. A condition can check the value of a field, or compare the value in the field to another value. When you use a condition, the macro will follow one of two paths depending on whether the condition is true or false.

**Example:**

> You might want a macro to perform certain tasks only when a given condition is true. For instance, you might want the macro to check a specified field to see if it is filled in; if not, the macro executes commands that prevent you from saving the record.

### Validating Data with Macros

Instead of attaching the macro to a specific control object on a form, you attach the macro to the form itself. That way, it does not matter where the person adding the record moves the focus, the macro will always run.

**Common Event Properties**

> The most common event properties to trigger data validation are included in the following table. The table details when a macro will execute if it is attached to this event.

# Lesson 4

| Event | Event Property | The Macro Will Execute |
|---|---|---|
| Record data is changed. | Before Update | Before the entered data is updated. |
| Changed record data is saved. | After Update | After the entered data is updated. |
| A new record is inserted. | Before Insert | After you type into a new record. |
| A record is deleted. | On Delete | In response to a deletion request, but before the record is deleted. |

When validating data, the macro is likely to contain the macro actions in the following table.

| Action | Use this Action To |
|---|---|
| Cancel Event | Prevent a user from posting a new record unless certain conditions are met. |
| Go To Control | Specify where on the form the insertion point is to be placed. |
| MsgBox | Display a custom message box. |

## Plan a Macro

Before actually creating a macro, you should plan what it will do. When planning, ask yourself:

### Guidelines

- What action by the user will trigger the macro?
- What is the first thing the macro will do? The second?
- Which control will trigger the macro?
- Which event property will trigger the macro?
- When will you want this macro to run?

### Example:

Figure 4-1 shows a flow chart illustrating the plan for a macro. Drawing a flow chart can help make your plan clear and easy to follow.

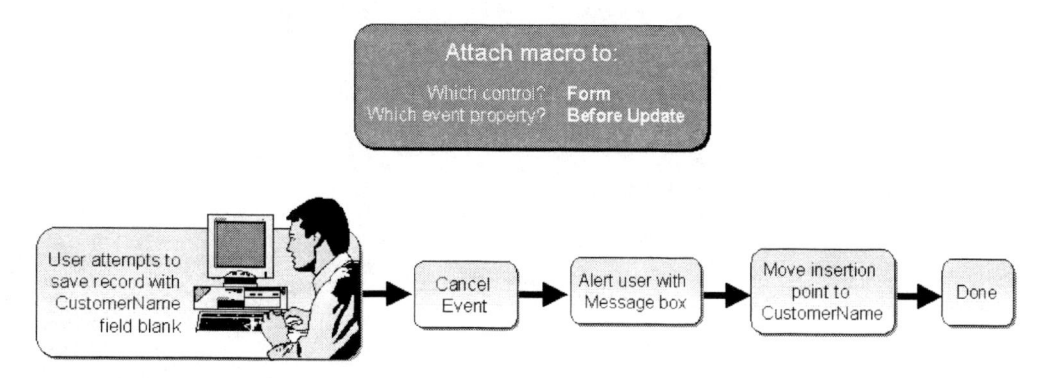

**Figure 4-1:** *A flow chart plan for a macro.*

Lesson 4: Adding Interaction and Automation with Macros

# Lesson 4

# ACTIVITY 4-1

## Planning a Macro that Requires Data Entry in a Field

**Scenario:**

The Customer Service manager is having a quality problem with her data entry representatives. Customer records are being entered into the CustomerRecord form with a blank CustomerName field. When it's time to ship products or access the customer record for any other reason, the lack of a customer name makes things difficult. The Customer Service Manager has come to you for help because she knows you're an Access expert. You decide to add a macro to the form that will prevent the record from being saved with a blank CustomerName field. Before you create this macro, you decide to spend some time planning it. The flow chart in Figure 4-1 illustrates what the planned macro will do. With your plan in hand, you can be more efficient in building your macro.

| What You Do | How You Do It |
|---|---|

1. What action by the user should trigger this macro?

2. What is the first thing the macro should do?

3. What is the second thing the macro should do?

4. What is the third thing the macro should do?

5. Which control can trigger this macro?

   You should attach the macro to the entire form and not to an individual control on the form. This ensures that the macro will run, even if the user never moves the insertion point to the specific control object.

6. Which event property can trigger this macro when you need to use it?

7. When will you want this macro to run?

# How to Require Data Entry with a Macro

**Procedure Reference: Require Data Entry With a Macro**

To require data entry with a macro:

1. On the desired form, from the Before Update property box, open the Macro builder.
2. Open the Condition column.
3. Create an Is Null condition for the appropriate field.
4. Enter a CancelEvent action.
5. Save the macro.

## Types of Macros

Typically, macros on forms can be grouped into categories according to their function; the macros in each category contain unique instructions that enable them to perform the indicated tasks.

- Validating data: You can create a macro to require that data be entered in a control, or to display a custom dialog box that prompts the user for additional information.
- Setting values: A powerful use for macros in a form is to have a macro set values for a control, field, or property. This can make data entry easier and more accurate.
- Navigating between forms and records: This type of macro moves to a specific control, record, or page in a form.
- Filtering, finding, and printing records: These types of macros automate the processes of filtering, finding, and printing records. A custom dialog box can be displayed to initiate the process specific to the user's needs.

# LESSON 4

# ACTIVITY 4-2

## Creating a Macro to Require Data Entry in a Field

### Data Files:

- Interaction.mdb

### Scenario:

Now that you have planned out your macro, it is time to actually build it. The macro you want to create will not allow a record to be saved without data in the CustomerName field. It will also return the insertion point to this field if an attempt to save is made while the field remains blank.

| What You Do | How You Do It |
|---|---|
| 1. With the frmCustomerRecord form opened in Design view, **display the Event page** of the Properties window for the form. | a. In Interaction.mdb, **open the frmCustomerRecord form in Design view.** <br><br> b. **Click the Properties button and verify that you have opened the Properties sheet for the form.** <br><br> c. **Select the Event tab.** |
| 2. In the Before Update property box, **open the Macro Builder. Name the macro *mcrMyRequireData*.** | a. **Click the Before Update property box.** <br><br> b. **Click the Build button.** <br><br> c. From the window, **choose Macro Builder and click OK.** <br><br> d. **Type *mcrMyRequireData* and click OK.** |

*Microsoft® Office Access 2003: Level 3*

# LESSON 4

3. **Display the Condition column.** In the first row of the Comment column, **enter the text** *To require data entry in the CustomerName field.*

   In the second row of the Condition column, **enter the text** *[CustomerName] is Null.*

   **Size the Condition column so you can read the full expression.**

   a. **Click the Conditions button** so that the Conditions column is now displayed.

   b. In the first row of the Comment column, **type** *To require data entry in the CustomerName field.*

   c. In the second row of the Condition column, **type** *[CustomerName] is Null*

   Be sure to enclose the field name in brackets and include a space between the words. **Press Enter.**

   ⚠ Do not type a period at the end of the conditional expression.

   d. **Double-click the Condition column border** to size the column, so you can see the entire condition as you work.

   ⚠ Double-clicking the column border does not work unless the condition has been entered. If you do not press Enter, you can drag the right column border to widen the column.

4. In the second row of the Action column, **choose CancelEvent.** In the second row of the Comment column, **type** *If CustomerName is left blank, do not save the record.*

   a. In the second row of the Action column, **select CancelEvent from the drop-down list.**

   b. In the second row of the Comment column, **type** *If CustomerName is left blank, do not save the record.*

*Lesson 4: Adding Interaction and Automation with Macros*

# Lesson 4

5. In the third row of the Condition column, **type ....** In the third row of the Action column, **choose GoToControl and type *[CustomerName]* in the Control Name field.** In the third row of the Comment column, **type *go to the CustomerName field*.**

   a. In the third row of the Condition column, **type ...** (entering an ellipsis (...) in the Condition column enables you to attach multiple actions to one condition).

   b. In the third row of the Action column, **select GoToControl from the drop-down list.**

   c. In the Action Arguments pane, in the Control Name text box, **type *[CustomerName]***

   d. In the Comment column for the third row, **type *Go to the CustomerName field*.**

6. **Save and close the macro and its Properties sheet, and then save the form as *frmMyCustomerRecord*.**

   a. **Click the Save button, and close the Macro window.** The macro is attached to the Before Update property.

   b. **Close the form's Properties window.**

   c. **Save the form as *frmMyCustomerRecord***

---

*[Handwritten notes:]*

On the form properties → before update → put macro.

Create → macro says :

| condition | Action |
|-----------|--------|
| field name | Msg box |
| ... | Cancel event |
| ... | Go to Control |

# Lesson 4

7. In Form view, **test the macro by entering a new record with the following data:**

    **Customer Number:** 303
    **Address:** 15 West Avenue
    **City:** Toronto
    **Region:** Ontario
    **Country:** Canada
    **Postal Code:** J2D 4T1
    **Phone:** 7853217734
    **Fax:** 7853231225

    a. In Form view, **click the New Record button.**

    b. In the Customer Number field, **type *303* and then press Tab twice** to leave the CustomerName field blank.

    c. **Enter the following data for the remaining fields:**

    **Customer Number:** 303
    **Address:** 15 West Avenue
    **City:** Toronto
    **Region:** Ontario
    **Country:** Canada
    **Postal Code:** J2D 4T1
    **Phone:** 7853217734
    **Fax:** 7853231225

    d. **Click the New Record button.**

8. What happens when you try to advance to a new record?


9. **Close the form without saving the record.**

    a. **Close the form.**

    b. **Click Yes.**

10. A dialog box indicates that you are unable to save the new record. Why?


*Lesson 4: Adding Interaction and Automation with Macros*     65

# LESSON 4

# TOPIC B

# Display a Message Box with a Macro

You have created a macro that prevents database users from saving customer records that do not contain a customer name. Even though they are not able to save, it may not be apparent to the user why. Giving the user feedback would help them to better understand. Next, you'll add a *message box* that advises users why their record cannot be saved.

You've probably had times where you have been working away at your computer when suddenly you couldn't perform the operation you were attempting, which is very frustrating. You may check the help files, or keep trying different approaches to get your work done. All the while, you wonder "What am I doing wrong?" It would be great if your computer could answer you. Adding a message box to the macro you created to require data entry will do just that for your database users.

## How to Display a Message Box with a Macro

**Procedure Reference: Modify an Existing Macro to Display a Message Box**

To modify an existing macro to display a message box:

1. Open the macro in Design view.
2. Insert a new row in the macro.
3. In the Action column of the new row, choose MsgBox.
4. In the Action Arguments pane, add message text, select a type, and enter a title.
5. Add comments.
6. Save your changes.

# ACTIVITY 4-3

## Modifying a Macro to Display a Message Box

### Setup:
Interaction.mdb is open.

### Scenario:
After testing out your macro to require data entry, you decide to add a message box. The message box will alert database users to the reason they cannot save their new record, and help make the adjustment to this new function more smooth.

| What You Do | How You Do It |
| --- | --- |
| 1. Open the mcrMyRequireData macro in Design view. Widen the Condition column, and then add a row above the third row in the macro. | a. In Design view, **open the mcrMyRequireData macro.**<br><br>b. **Double-click the Condition column border.**<br><br>c. In the third row of the macro, **right-click the Selector tab to the left of the Condition column.**<br><br>d. From the menu, **choose Insert Rows**. |
| 2. In the Condition column of the new row, **type ...** and **choose MsgBox in the Action column.** | a. In the Condition column of the new row, **type ...** (an ellipsis).<br><br>b. In the Action column of the new row, **select MsgBox from the drop-down list.** |

*Lesson 4: Adding Interaction and Automation with Macros*

# Lesson 4

3. In the Action Arguments pane, in the Message text box, **type *You must enter a value in the Customer Name field*.** In the Type box, **choose Information.** In the Title box, **type *Required Data*.**

    a. In the Action Arguments pane, in the Message box, **type *You must enter a value in the Customer Name field*.** This is the text that will be displayed in the message box.

    b. In the Type field, **select Information from the drop-down list.** This selects the Information icon for the message box.

    c. In the Title field, **type *Required Data***

    This will be the title for the message box.

4. Add the comment *...display a message box to inform the user why the record is not saved*. Save and close the macro.

    a. In the Comment column of the new row, type *...display a message box to inform the user why the record is not saved.*

    b. **Save your changes and close the Macro window.**

# TOPIC C

# Automate Data Entry

You've seen how you can use macros to require data entry and to communicate with database users. You can also use macros to speed up the data entry process. Instead of having users type in the same data over and over for each record, a macro can automate the entry of static information. Next, you'll see how you can use macros to automate parts of the data entry process.

Suppose you wanted to run a report that showed a listing of all customers in the state of California. Seems simple enough, but what if there were misspellings in the State field? Simple errors in data entry can have an impact on the accuracy of your reports. Automating data entry can help to ensure the quality of your data. For example, you could create a macro that automatically enters the country name based on the region entered. As a benefit to database users, this automation also saves data entry time.

## How to Automate Data Entry

### Procedure Reference: Specify a Condition for Automating Data Entry

To specify a condition for automating data entry:

1. Select a field to which you want to attach the condition.
2. From the Properties window, select the appropriate event.
3. Start the Macro Builder.

4. Click the Conditions button to make the Conditions field visible.
5. Apply the appropriate conditions to automate data entry.

## Events and Actions for Automating Data Entry

Macros can help you to reduce errors in data entry and to make data entry easier and more efficient. By creating a macro that sets the value of one field based on the value of another, you can reduce the amount of typing needed to enter records. Although you can set a field's default value at the table level or in a form, using a macro gives you more control and flexibility when the validation of data involves more than one value on the form. You can also use macros to compare values from different tables, unbound values, or values in tables from other database applications.

You can attach macros to the form or to individual controls. When you attach a macro to a control, the macro takes effect against the control. For example, you can set a data value at the field level (rather than when the record is exited) by using the field's Before Update property, rather than the property at the form level.

| Event | Event Property | The Macro will Execute |
| --- | --- | --- |
| A control is selected. | On Enter | Upon arriving on a control, but before the control has focus. |
| Control data is changed. | Before Update | Before the control data is updated. |
| A changed control is updated. | After Update | After the changed control data is updated. |
| A control is left. | On Exit | Upon leaving a control, but before the focus is removed. |

When you intend to set values with a macro, it is likely that you will use the macro actions in the following table.

| Action | Use this Action To |
| --- | --- |
| SetValue | To enter a specified value in a field. In the Action Arguments pane, specify the field name in which you would like the value entered (Item) and the actual value you want entered (Expression). |
| GoToControl | To specify where on the form the insertion point is to be placed. |

*Lesson 4: Adding Interaction and Automation with Macros*

# Lesson 4

## Activity 4-4

### Creating a Macro that will Run Under Specific Conditions

**Setup:**
Interaction.mdb is open.

**Scenario:**
The Customer Service manager is thrilled with the macros you have created to remind data entry representatives to input customer names. Now that she sees the potential of macros, she has another request. She would like you to create a macro that will automatically input Canada in the Country Name field if Alberta or Ontario is entered into the Region field and then move the insertion point onto the next field.

| What You Do | How You Do It |
|---|---|
| 1. From the Property window for the Region field of frmMyCustomerRecord, **open the Macro Builder from the On Exit property box and create a new macro named** *mcrMyDefaultValue*. | a. From the Design view of frmMyCustomerRecord, **select the Region text box control and click the Properties button.**<br><br>b. From the Event page, **select the On Exit event and click the Build button.**<br><br>c. From the window, **select Macro Builder, and create a new macro named** *mcrMyDefaultValue* |
| 2. **Display the Conditions column,** and in the first row of the Comment column, **type** *To enter a value in Country based on the value in Region.* | a. **Click the Conditions button.**<br><br>b. In the first row of the Comment column, **type** *To enter a value in Country based on the value in Region.* |

3. In the second row of the macro, **use the SetValue action to automatically enter Canada in the Country field when either Alberta or Ontario is entered into the Region field. In the Comment field, type *If Region is Alberta or Ontario, set Country to Canada.***

a. In the second row of the Condition column, **type *[Region] in ("Alberta","Ontario")***

b. In the second row of the Action column, **choose SetValue.**

c. In the Action Arguments pane, **enter the following:**
   - **Item:** `[Country]`
   - **Expression:** `"Canada"`

d. In the second row of the Comment column, **type *If Region is Alberta or Ontario, set Country to Canada.***

*Lesson 4: Adding Interaction and Automation with Macros*

# Lesson 4

4. In the third row, **use the GoToControl action so that the cursor will jump to the Postal Code field. Add a comment reading** ...*go to the PostalCode field.*

   a. In the third row of the Conditions column, **type ...** to indicate that you would like to attach another action to the original condition.

   b. In the third row of the Action column, **choose GoToControl.**

   c. In the Action Arguments pane, in the Control Name text box, **type *[PostalCode]*** to specify to which control you want the insertion point to move. (You must include brackets around the name of the specified control.)

   d. In the third row of the Comment column, **type** ...*go to the PostalCode field.*

   e. The macro is now complete. **Save and close the Macro window.**

   f. The Properties sheet shows that the new macro has been attached to the Region field's On Exit event. **Close the Properties sheet.**

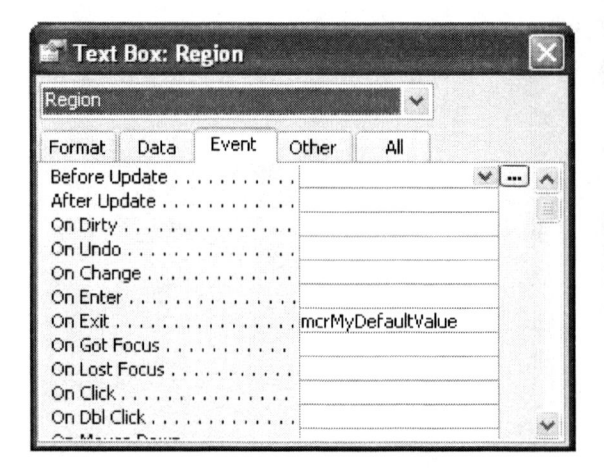

# Lesson 4

5. **Test the macro in Form view by entering a new record with the following data:**

   **Customer Number:** 367
   **Customer Name:** The Hitching Rail
   **Address:** 455 Creek Rd.
   **City:** Huntsville
   **Region:** Ontario
   **Postal Code:** THX138
   **Phone:** 7874443892
   **Fax:** 7874443855

   **Save and close the database.**

   a. In Form view, **click the New Record button.**

   b. **Enter the following values:**
      **Customer Number:** 367
      **Customer Name:** The Hitching Rail
      **Address:** 455 Creek Rd.
      **City:** Huntsville
      **Region:** Ontario

   c. **Press Tab.** When Ontario is entered in the Region field, the value Canada is automatically entered into the Country field, and the focus moves to the Postal Code field.

   d. **Complete the form with the following values:**
      **Postal Code:** THX138
      **Phone:** 7874443892
      **Fax:** 7874443855

   e. **Press Shift+Enter** to save the record.

   f. **Save and close the database.**

# Lesson 4 Follow-up

In this lesson, you added interaction and automation with macros. Using macros in this way will allow you better control of the information entered in your database. Macros can also communicate with and guide the end users.

1. **Can you think of any forms you've created that could benefit from a message box? Explain.**

2. **How might requiring data entry help when creating forms in the future?**

*Lesson 4: Adding Interaction and Automation with Macros*

# Notes

# LESSON 5
# Making Forms More Effective

**Lesson Time**
*45 minutes*

## Lesson Objectives:

In this lesson, you will improve the effectiveness of data entry in forms.

You will:

- Use conditional formatting to change the appearance of a control as the data changes.
- Display a calendar on a form.
- Use a Tab control on a form to organize the display of information.

# LESSON 5

## Introduction

Most databases contain many forms, some for data entry and others for viewing the data. This lesson shows you a few techniques you may not have tried before that can enhance the usability of your forms and the productivity of the database users.

Forms are what most users see and work with every day. As you learn more about the capabilities of forms, you'll be able to build in more functionality and save users time and work.

# TOPIC A

## Change the Display of Data Conditionally

Up until now, all your focus when working with forms has been to get the data into the correct tables. Sometimes, however, you might just want to draw the user's attention to a particular control or value on a form. In this topic, you will change the format of a control based on a condition you set.

The users of forms are only human and all humans make mistakes. The number of errors can increase when people are hurried or distracted. Anything you, as a form designer, can do to make sure that users notice important information will help reduce errors in your business. Changing the display of a form based on the data a user enters allows you to provide immediate feedback about the information they just entered. For example, you could change the associated text to red to indicate that the previously entered data was unacceptable in that field.

## Conditional Formatting

**Definition:**

> *Conditional formatting* is an Access tool that enables you to change the formatting of a control based on conditions that you define. You can set up to three conditions. Conditional formatting can be used in forms and reports.

**Example:**

> You can use conditional formatting to change the font or color of the data displayed in a control or to make it bold, italic, or underlined. You can also change the background color of a control or enable or disable it.

## How to Change the Display of Data Conditionally

**Procedure Reference: Apply Conditional Formatting to a Control**

> To apply conditional formatting to a control:
>
> 1. Select the control.
> 2. Choose Format→Conditional Formatting.
> 3. Enter the condition(s) under which the formatting is to be applied.

4. Select the formatting you want to apply.
5. Click OK.

# ACTIVITY 5-1

## Applying Conditional Formatting

**Data Files:**

- Forms.mdb

**Scenario:**
In the Forms database, you created the frmCategories form for Customer Service representatives to use when customers call to inquire about the pricing of products in certain categories. The Customer Service representatives are also supposed to point out to customers the items that carry additional shipping charges, but they often forget to do so. The company applies extra shipping charges to items with a unit price of $100 or more; you just need to create a way to draw attention to those items.

| What You Do | How You Do It |
|---|---|
| 1. In Forms.mdb, in the design of the frmCategories form, **add conditional formatting to the Price text box that will display its values in red when the value is equal to or greater than $100.** | a. Open the database Forms.mdb.<br><br>b. Open frmCategories in Design view.<br><br>c. Select the Price text box.<br><br>d. Choose Format→Conditional Formatting.<br><br>e. In the Condition1 box, **verify that the first text box contains Field Value Is.**<br><br>f. From the second drop-down list, **select Greater Than Or Equal To.**<br><br>g. In the third text box, **type 100** |

**LESSON 5**

*Lesson 5: Making Forms More Effective*

# Lesson 5

        h. From the Font/Fore Color palette, **choose red**.

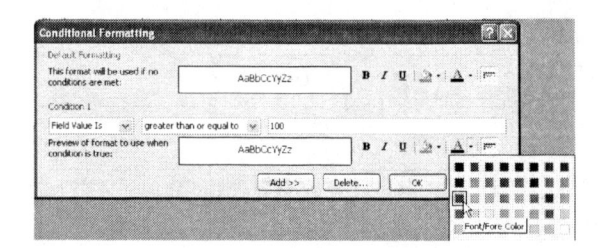

        i. **Click OK.**

2. **Apply the same conditional formatting to the Product text box.** Note that the name of the main form is frmCategories and the subform is fsubProducts.

        a. **Click the Product text box.**

        b. **Choose Format→Conditional Formatting.**

        c. In the Condition1 box, from the first drop-down list, **select Expression Is.**

        d. In the second text box, **type the code seen in the following sample.**

           *See Code Sample 1.*

        e. From the Font/Fore Color palette, **select red.**

        f. **Click OK.**

## Code Sample 1

```
[Price]>=100
```

3. **Switch to Form view and test the conditional formatting. Save and close the form.**

        a. **Switch to Form view.**

        b. **Advance through the existing records, noting the records in red.**

        c. **Save and close the form.**

# TOPIC B

# Display a Calendar on a Form

You have used many different types of controls on your forms, but just using simple controls will keep you from taking advantage of advanced tools, such as a calendar. A calendar is a very useful control that can be on many different forms. In this topic, you will display a calendar on a form.

When working closely with dates, having a calendar nearby is very helpful. Instead of using a paper calendar or switching to another program to check dates, you can just include a calendar right on your form.

## How to Display a Calendar on a Form

### Procedure Reference: Add a Calendar Control to a Form

To add a calendar control to a form:

1. Open the form in Design view.
2. In the Toolbox, click the More Controls tool.
3. From the list, select the control you wish to add.
4. Click the form where you want to create the control.

### Form Properties

A form has a number of Format properties that can be set to control its appearance. The most commonly used properties are summarized in the following table; the default setting for each property is indicated by an asterisk (*).

| Property | Settings |
| --- | --- |
| Default View | Single Form*, Continuous Forms, Datasheet, PivotTable, PivotChart |
| Scroll Bars | Neither, Horizontal Only, Vertical Only, Both* |
| Record Selectors | Yes*, No |
| Navigation Buttons | Yes*, No |
| Dividing Lines | Yes*, No |
| Border Style | None, Thin, Sizable*, Dialog |
| Control Box | Yes*, No |
| Min Max Buttons | None, Min Enabled, Max Enabled, Both Enabled* |
| Close Button | Yes*, No |
| What's This Button | Yes, No* |

The BorderStyle settings are explained in the following table.

Lesson 5: Making Forms More Effective

# Lesson 5

| Setting | Description |
|---|---|
| None | Form has no border or border elements; not resizable. |
| Thin | Form has a thin border and can include any of the border elements; not resizable. |
| Sizable | Form has the default border for Access forms and can include any of the border elements; resizable. |
| Dialog | Form has a thick border and can only have a title bar, Close button, and Control box; not resizable. |

# Activity 5-2

## Displaying a Calendar on a Form

**Setup:**
Forms.mdb is open.

**Scenario:**
You created the frmOrders form to be used for order entry. The supervisor of the Customer Service group tells you that the people taking orders often need to refer to a calendar to answer customer questions, such as when they will receive a shipment. A calendar is needed so the Customer Service people can take weekends and holidays into account when they make the estimate.

| What You Do | How You Do It |
|---|---|
| 1. Create a new form and place a Calendar Control 11.0 on it. Check how it looks in Form view. | a. From the Forms tab, **create a new form in Design view**. |
| | b. In the Toolbox, **click the More Controls button**. |
| | c. **Select Calendar Control 11.0.** |
| | d. **Click the blank form to create the calendar.** |
| | e. **Switch to Form view.** |

2. **Set the appropriate properties so the form will have:**
   - A dialog box style border.
   - No scroll bars.
   - No record selectors.
   - No navigation buttons.
   - No dividing lines.
   - A caption of *Lone Pine Calendar*.

   Size the control, the form, and the window. Save it as *frmMyCalendar* and view the form.

   a. **Switch to Design view.**

   b. **Open the Form Properties sheet and select the Format tab.**

   c. In the Caption text box, **type** *Lone Pine Calendar*

   d. **Set the Scroll Bars property to Neither.**

   e. **Set the Record Selectors property to No.**

   f. **Set the Navigation Buttons property to No.**

   g. **Set the Dividing Lines property to No.**

   h. **Set the Border Style property to Dialog.**

   i. If you wish, **size the Calendar control and size the form and the window to fit the control.**

   j. **Save the form as *frmMyCalendar* and switch to Form view.**

3. **What other changes might you want to make to the appearance of the form or the calendar?**

*Lesson 5: Making Forms More Effective*

# Lesson 5

4. After making any sizing changes you want, **set the Calendar control properties so the full name of the month is displayed and the current date is not selected. Check your settings by viewing the form.**

   a. **Switch to Design view.**

   b. **Select the Calendar control.**

   c. In the Properties sheet, **select the Other tab.**

   d. **Set the MonthLength property to English.**

   e. **Set the ValueIsNull property to Yes.**

   f. **Close the Properties window.**

   g. **Switch to Form view.**

   h. **Save and close the form.**

# Lesson 5

5. Place a command button on frmOrders that opens the myCalendar form and displays a caption of *Show Calendar*.

   Test the button.

   a. Open frmOrders in Design view.

   b. With Control Wizards selected in the Toolbox, **add a command button control.**

   c. In the Categories list, **select Form Operations.** In the Actions list, **select Open Form. Click Next.**

   d. From the list of forms, **select frmMyCalendar and click Next.**

   e. **Select the Text option and type** *Show Calendar*

   **Click Next.**

   f. In the name text box, **type** *cmdCalendar*

   **Click Finish.**

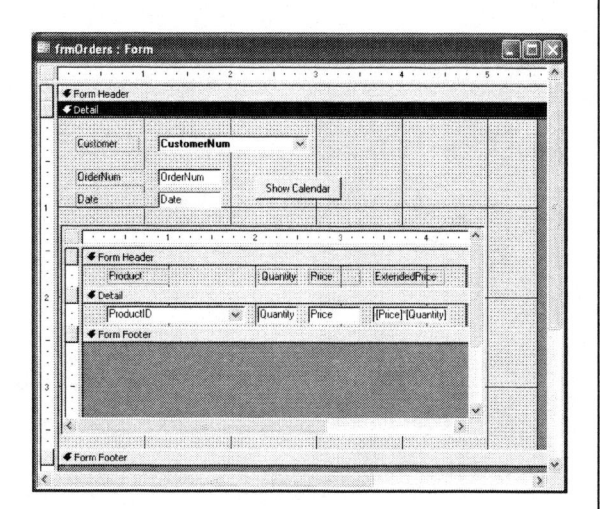

   g. **Switch to Form view and test the button.**

*Lesson 5: Making Forms More Effective*

# Lesson 5

6. **Create a new macro that will open the myCalendar form at a position 5 inches to the right on the screen. Save the macro as *mcrCalendar* and link it to the cmdCalendar button.**

   📌 *Depending on the size and resolution of your computer monitor, 5 inches to the right may not be the best position. You can revise the setting and test it again.*

   a. **Save and close any open forms.**

   b. From the database window, **start a new macro.**

   c. In the first Action row, **select OpenForm and set the Form Name argument to frmMyCalendar.**

   d. In the second Action row, **select MoveSize and set the Right argument to *5***

   e. **Save the macro as *mcrCalendar* and close it.**

   f. **Display frmOrders in Design view.**

   g. In the OnClick property of the cmdCalendar button, **change the setting from [Event Procedure] to mcrCalendar.**

   h. **Save the form and test the command button.**

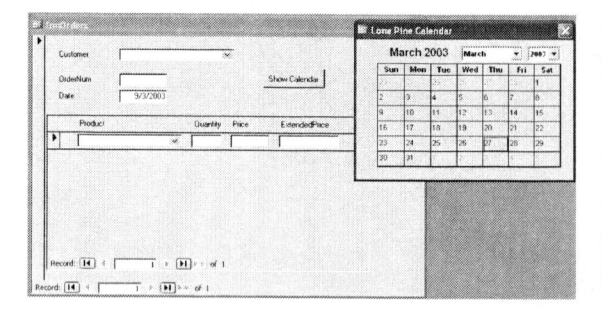

   i. **Close both forms.**

# Topic C

## Organize Information with Tab Pages

You may have used boxes, lines, and other features to help draw the user's eye to certain groupings of data on forms. Another way to organize information on a form is to use *tab pages*. In this topic, you will use tab pages.

Rather than users having to open several different forms to view different sets of information, you can make their work more efficient by providing one form with tab pages. This enables you to place more data on a single form and allows the users easier access to what they need.

## Tab Pages

**Definition:**

A tab page is an Access control that allows you to create multiple pages on one form. Each page is separated by its own tab. You can use the same controls on a tab page that you would use when creating a single page form.

**Example:**

Figure 5-1 is an example of a tab page.

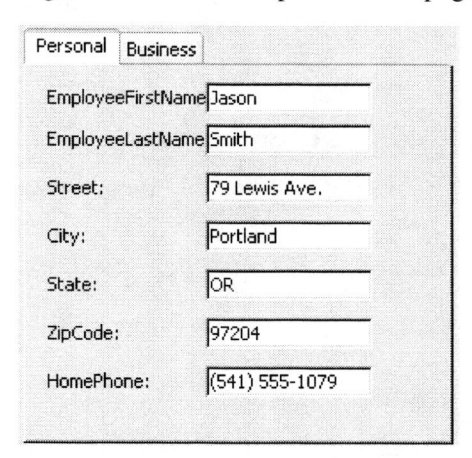

**Figure 5-1:** *Tab pages on a form.*

## How to Organize Information with Tab Pages

**Procedure Reference: Create a New Form with Tab Pages**

To create a new form with tab pages:

1. Create a new form in Design view.
2. Select the form and set the Record Source property.
3. In the Toolbox, click the Tab Control tool.
4. Click the form where you want to create the Tab control.
5. Set the Name property for each of the tabs.
6. Display the Field List and add the fields you want on each tab page.

# Lesson 5

7. Save the form.

# ACTIVITY 5-3

## Creating Tab Pages on a Form

**Setup:**
Forms.mdb is open.

**Scenario:**
You're having lunch with the manager of Human Resources, whose department also uses Access databases. You've been telling her about all the interesting things you've learned that you can do in Access to increase efficiency and usability. She mentions that HR currently has a lot of different forms in their database—each with a special purpose—and wonders if there's a better way to handle the data and avoid having to open and close so many forms. You reply that you've heard about Tab controls on forms and agree to build a new form for her to try out.

| What You Do | How You Do It |
| --- | --- |
| 1. How might you categorize the data in the qselEmployeeInfo query? | |
| 2. Create a new form with a record source of qselEmployeeInfo. Add a Tab control to the form. | a. Create a new form in Design view.<br><br>b. In the Properties window for the form, on the Data tab, **set the Record Source property to qselEmployeeInfo**.<br><br>c. In the Toolbox, **click the Tab Control tool**.<br><br>d. **Click the form** where you want the Tab control created. |

86  Microsoft® Office Access 2003: Level 3

# Lesson 5

3. **Change the caption of the Page1 tab to *Personal* and add the following fields:**
   - EmployeeFirstName
   - EmployeeLastName
   - Street
   - City
   - State
   - ZipCode
   - HomePhone

   📌 Don't spend too much time now sizing and aligning controls; you can come back and do that later, if you wish.

   a. If necessary, **select the Page1 tab of the Tab control.**

   📌 Click the actual tab to select the page.

   b. In the Properties sheet, **select the Format tab.**

   c. **Set the Caption property to *Personal***

   d. From the qselEmployeeInfo field list box, **drag the following fields to the Personal tab area:**
      - EmployeeFirstName
      - EmployeeLastName
      - Street
      - City
      - State
      - ZipCode
      - HomePhone

*Lesson 5: Making Forms More Effective*

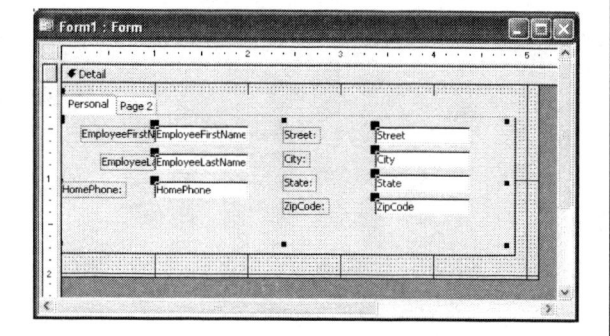

# Lesson 5

4. **Change the caption of the Page2 tab to *Company* and add the following fields:**
   - EmployeeFirstName
   - EmployeeLastName
   - DeptNum
   - DeptName
   - OfficeExt
   - HourlyRate
   - WeeklyHours
   - HealthIns

   **Save the form as *frmMyEmployeeInfo* View the form and test the tab pages.**

   a. **Select Page2 of the Tab control.**

   b. **Set the Caption property to *Company***

   c. **From the qselEmployeeInfo field list box, drag the following fields to the Company tab area:**
      - EmployeeFirstName
      - EmployeeLastName
      - DeptNum
      - DeptName
      - OfficeExt
      - HourlyRate
      - WeeklyHours
      - HealthIns

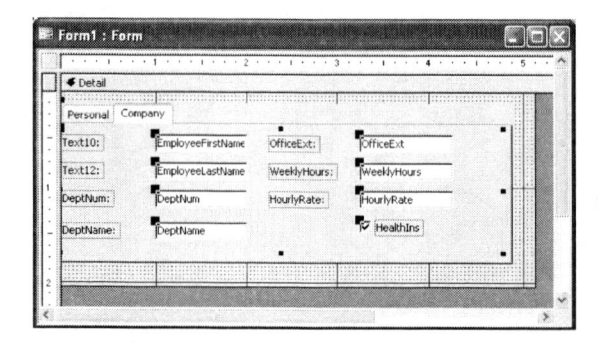

   d. **Save the form as *frmMyEmployeeInfo***

   e. **Switch to Form view and test the tab pages.**

5. Change the order of the pages so the Company page is displayed first. Change the style of the Tab control to Buttons. Save and close the database.

   a. Switch to Design view.

   b. Select the Tab control.

   c. Right-click the Tab control and choose Page Order.

   d. In the Page Order dialog box, **verify that Personal is selected and click Move Down. Click OK.**

   e. From the Tab Control properties window, on the Format tab, **change the Style property to Buttons.**

   f. Switch to Form view.

   g. Save and close the database.

# Lesson 5 Follow-up

In this lesson, you made your forms more effective. The more functionality you build into your forms, the easier and more time-saving it is for the end user.

1. **How do you plan to improve your existing forms?**

2. **Are there places in any of your existing databases where tab pages might be useful? Explain.**

*Lesson 5: Making Forms More Effective*

# Notes

# Lesson 6
# Making Reports More Effective

**Lesson Time**
*50 minutes*

## Lesson Objectives:

In this lesson, you will improve the effectiveness of data displayed in reports.

You will:

- Create a macro that cancels the printing of a report when empty.
- Add a chart to a report to increase its visual impact.
- Create a multi-column report that uses functions and operators to control the printing of data.
- Create a snapshot of a report so that it can be viewed without the Access program.

# Lesson 6

## Introduction

You've probably used the Report Wizard many times to create the foundation for your reports. But the wizard doesn't automatically provide some of the more powerful things you can do with *reports*. This lesson gets you started on creating customized reports.

Reports are your way of communicating database information throughout the company. This lesson shows you some techniques you can use to present your information in the most effective format.

# Topic A

## Cancel Printing of a Blank Report

You've probably created some fairly sophisticated reports and have made frequent use of parameters to have users input report criteria. However, if the user enters criteria for a report that doesn't exist, Access will create an empty report. In this topic, you will cancel the printing of a blank report.

If a report contains no records, the detail area of the report will be blank. If a user is accustomed to sending a report directly to a printer (rather than previewing it first), he or she won't find out it's blank until it is picked up from the printer. Aside from wasting paper, the user has wasted time. You can prevent this in the design of the report.

### How to Cancel Printing of a Blank Report

**Procedure Reference: Run a Macro to Cancel a Report That Contains No Records**

To run a macro to cancel a report that contains no records:

1. Open the report in Design view.
2. From the On No Data event property, click the Build button.
3. Run the Macro Builder.
4. Name the macro and click OK.
5. In the first Action row, select MsgBox from the drop-down list and set your arguments.
6. In the second Action row, choose the CancelEvent action.
7. Save and close the macro.
8. Save the report.

#### Report Events

You can use report events to run macros. The events for a report, along with descriptions and possible ways you might use them, are given in the following table.

| Event | Explanation | Possible Use |
|---|---|---|
| Open | Occurs before report is previewed or printed and before, if applicable, underlying query is run. | Open a custom dialog box to collect report criteria. |
| Close | Occurs when the report window is closed. | Display a menu or a switchboard form. |
| Activate | Occurs when the report window becomes the active window. | Show a custom toolbar or maximize the report window. |
| Deactivate | Occurs when the window loses the focus and before the Close event. | Hide a custom toolbar. |
| No Data | Occurs when the underlying query has been run with no records returned. | Cancel the previewing or printing of the report. |
| Page | Occurs after a report page has been formatted for printing but before it's printed. | Draw a border around the page. |
| Error | Occurs when there is a run-time error generated by the database engine. | Display a custom error message. |

# ACTIVITY 6-1

## Canceling the Printing of a Blank Report

### Data Files:

- Reports.mdb

### Scenario:

You're really quite proud of the report you created for the Customer Service group. Named rptCustomerOrders, it enables the Customer Service staff to print a report for the customer of their choice for the time period of their choice. The problem is that sometimes there are no customer orders for the time period they specify and the report detail is blank. You want to cancel printing in these cases.

| What You Do | How You Do It |
|---|---|

For the purposes of class, you will preview the report rather than actually sending it to a printer.

*Lesson 6: Making Reports More Effective*

# Lesson 6

1. Open Reports.mdb and preview the rptCustomerOrders report for the customer *The Happy Camper* for the period *3/1/01* through *3/6/01*.

    Review the content of the report, and then close it.

    Preview the report again for the same customer for the period *6/1/01* through *6/6/01*.

    Observe the blank report and then switch to Design view.

    a. Open Reports.mdb and preview the rptCustomerOrders report.

    b. Enter a Customer Name of *The Happy Camper*

    c. Enter a start date of *3/1/01* and an end date of *3/6/01*

    d. Review the content of the report and close when finished.

    e. Preview the report again for the same customer with a start date of *6/1/01* and an end date of *6/6/01*

    Notice that the report contains no data.

    f. Switch to Design view.

2. Start the Macro Builder for the report's On No Data event. Create a macro named myNoData that will display the message *There were no orders during the period specified* in an Information type message box with *Lone Pine Outfitters* in the title bar. Include an action to cancel printing (or previewing) of the report. Save the macro and close the macro window.

    a. Open the Properties sheet.

    b. Select the Event page.

    c. Click the Build button for the On No Data event and start the Macro Builder.

    d. Enter a macro name of *myNoData* and click OK.

    e. Close the Properties window.

    f. In the first Action row, **select the MsgBox action.**

    g. In the Action Arguments pane, **set the following arguments:**
    - Message: There were no orders during the period specified
    - Type: Information
    - Title: Lone Pine Outfitters

    h. In the second Action row, **select the CancelEvent action.**

    i. Save and close the macro.

94                                      Microsoft® Office Access 2003: Level 3

3. Save and close the report. Test the macro by attempting to preview the report for the customer *The Happy Camper* for the period *6/1/01* through *6/6/01*.

a. Save and close the report.

b. Preview the rptCustomerOrders report and enter the following parameters:
- CustomerName: The Happy Camper
- Start date: 6/1/01
- End date: 6/6/01

c. When your message box is displayed, **click OK.**

# TOPIC B

# Include a Chart in a Report

You've created a lot of reports and you've seen how a PivotChart can be used on a form or with a query. But when you don't need the interactivity of a PivotChart and just want a chart to be part of your printed output, you can use the Chart Wizard to add a graph to a report. In this topic, you will include a chart in a report.

The printed output of reports may be all the evidence that some users see of all your hard work on your database. Making those reports professional-looking will enhance the impression made on the consumers. Also, some people respond better to a graphical representation of data, so a chart will give them what they need.

## How to Include a Chart in a Report

### Procedure Reference: Add a Chart to a Report Using the Chart Wizard

To add a chart to a report using the Chart Wizard:

1. Open the report in Design view.
2. Choose Insert→Chart.
3. Click in the report to create the control and start the wizard.
4. Select the data source for the chart.
5. Select the fields you want to chart.
6. Select the chart type.
7. Select whether you want the chart to change from record to record.
8. Enter a title for the chart and finish the wizard.
9. Save the report.

*Lesson 6: Making Reports More Effective*

# LESSON 6

# ACTIVITY 6-2

## Adding a Chart to a Report

**Setup:**

Reports.mdb is open.

**Scenario:**

You've created a summary report, rptQ1CategorySales (based on the qselQ1CategorySales query), that shows the first quarter's total sales for each product in each category, total sales for each category, and a grand total. You would like to make the comparison of category sales more obvious by adding a chart to the report. You want the chart to show just the total for each category, so you created qtotCategories to produce that data.

| What You Do | How You Do It |
|---|---|
| 1. **Preview all pages of the rptQ1CategorySales report, and then switch to Design view.** | a. From the Reports tab, **double-click rptQ1CategorySales.** |
| | b. **Click the Next Record button** to advance to the second page. |
| | c. **Switch to Design view.** |

2. Insert a pie chart in the report footer, basing the chart on the qtotCategories query. The chart should not change from record to record and will have a title of *Q1 Category Sales*.

   a. Enlarge the report footer to approximately 2.5 inches high.

   b. Choose Insert→Chart.

   c. In the report footer, **click to create a Chart control.**

   d. From the Chart Wizard, **click the Queries radio button and select Query: qtotCategories. Click Next.**

   e. **Add both fields to the chart and click Next.**

   f. From the thumbnails of chart types, **select Pie Chart and click Next.**

   g. **Click the Preview Chart button** to examine the chart before it is created.

   h. **Close the preview and click Next.**

   i. From the first drop-down list in both the Report Fields and Chart fields, **select No Field. Click Next.**

   j. **Give the chart a title of *Q1 Category Sales* and click Finish.**

3. Preview the report and the chart. Save the report as *rptMyQ1CategorySalesReport*, and then close the report.

   a. Preview the report and view the chart on the second page.

   b. Save the report as *rptMyQ1CategorySalesReport*

   c. Close the report.

*Lesson 6: Making Reports More Effective*

# Lesson 6

## Topic C

# Arrange Data in Columns

You may have had to deal with the issue of trying to squeeze all the fields of data you need into the width of a report. But it is also possible to have the opposite problem of having just a few fields and, as a result, the report has too much white space. This topic will show you how you can arrange your fields of data in multiple columns on the page.

Some of your reports may involve long lists of just a few fields of data—like a phone or product list. These may be best arranged in multiple columns for readability and so you don't waste many pages of paper.

## How to Arrange Data in Columns

### Procedure Reference: Create a Multiple-column Report

To create a multiple-column report:

1. Create a new report in Design view.
2. Place the controls you want to print in each column within your chosen width in the Detail section.
3. Add a group header and/or footer.
4. Choose File→Page Setup and select the Columns page.
5. Enter the number of columns and column spacing.
6. Select the column width.
7. Select the column layout and click OK.
8. Save the report.

# ACTIVITY 6-3

## Printing Data in Columns

**Setup:**

Reports.mdb is open.

**Scenario:**

You've been asked to produce an internal phone list from the company's Human Resources database. You would like it to be highly readable with some type of divider for easy reference and to fit on one page so people can post it on the wall near their phones. You've already created the qselPhoneList query that extracts the EmployeeLastName, EmployeeFirstName, and OfficeExt fields and puts the records in alphabetical order, so that should be a good starting point.

| What You Do | How You Do It |
|---|---|
| 1. **Create a new report in Design view and make qselPhoneList the record source. Add a page heading of** *Lone Pine Phone List* **with a font size of 24.** | a. From the Reports tab, **click the New button.** |
| | b. From the New Report wizard, **select Design View from the list and set the Record Source property to qselPhoneList. Click OK.** |
| | c. **Add a Label control to the Page Header.** |
| | d. In the Label control, **type** *Lone Pine Internal Phone List* |
| | e. From the Properties sheet, **change the font size to 24.** |

*Lesson 6: Making Reports More Effective*

# Lesson 6

2. In the Detail section, **add a control that will print names in the format of "last name comma space first name."** Add the OfficeExt field and delete the Label controls associated with both text boxes. Place the controls towards the left side of the report.

   a. In the left side of the Detail section, **add a Text Box control and delete its associated label.**

   b. In the Control Source property for the new text box, **type =[EmployeeLastName]&","&[EmployeeFirstName]**

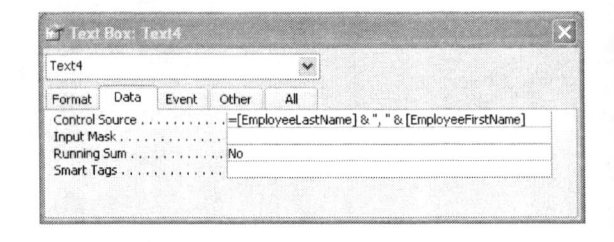

   *Due to margin constraints, what you need to type in this step had to be put on two separate lines. Please make sure that when you are typing this control, you do not add any spaces.*

   c. From the field list, **drag the OfficeExt field to the left side of the Detail section and delete its associated label.**

3. **Add a group header for the expression that will extract the first letter of each last name.** Since you will use it again, **copy the expression to the clipboard. Set the Keep Together property for the group to Whole Group.**

   a. **Click the Sorting And Grouping button.**

   b. In the first Field/Expression row, **type =Left([EmployeeLastName],1)** and copy the expression to the clipboard.

   *As an alternative, you could group the report on the EmployeeLastName field and set the Group on property to Prefix Characters. Confirm the Group Interval property is set to 1. This will create a group based on the first letter of the employee's last name.*

   c. In the Group Properties pane, **set the Group Header property to Yes.**

# LESSON 6

   d. **Set the Keep Together property to Whole Group.**

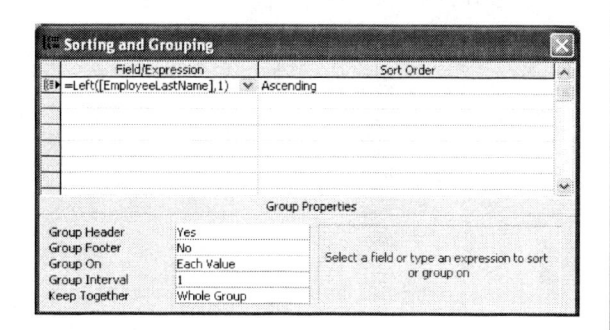

   e. **Close the Sorting And Grouping dialog box.**

4. On the left side of the new group header, **add a Text Box control and paste in the expression from the clipboard. Increase the font size to 10.**

   a. On the left side of the Group Header section, **add a Text Box control and delete its associated label.**

   b. In the Control Source property box for the text box, **paste the expression from the clipboard.**

   c. **Change the font size to 10.**

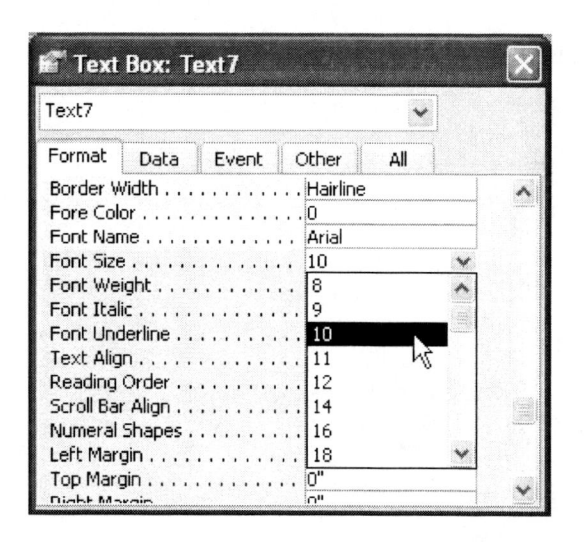

*Lesson 6: Making Reports More Effective*     101

# LESSON 6

5. Using the Page Setup dialog box, set the number of columns to *2*, the column spacing to *0.5*, and the column width to *3* inches. Make sure the data will print in snaking columns down the page. Size the report sections. Preview the report and see if the data fits on one page.

   a. **Choose File→Page Setup.**

   b. On the Columns page, in the Grid Settings box, **set Number Of Columns to *2* and set Column Spacing to *0.5***

   c. In the Column Size box, **uncheck Same As Detail and enter a Width of *3***

   d. In the Column Layout box, **select Down, Then Across.**

   e. **Click OK.**

   f. Drag the Page Footer bar up so that it is right below the Detail section text boxes.

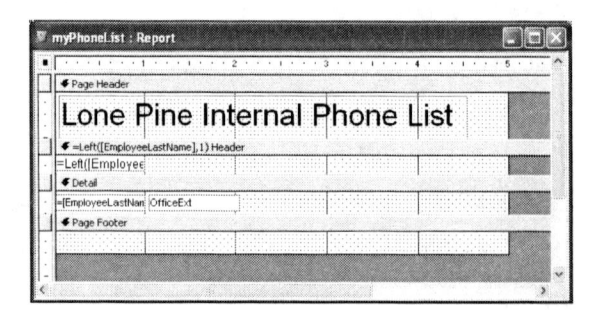

   g. **Preview the report.**

6. If your report is not on one page, what are some techniques you can use to make it more compact?

   _____

7. Save the report as *myPhoneList* and close the report.

   a. Save the report as *myPhoneList*

   b. **Close the report.**

# Topic D

# Create a Report Snapshot

Reports often contain valuable information that needs to be accessible to all employees—or even people outside the company. A report snapshot enables you to reach a wider audience, thereby enhancing communication in an efficient way. In this topic, you will distribute reports as a snapshot.

Printing and copying Access reports is the most common way of distributing the information they contain to many people. But that can be time consuming and expensive and, unless you have a color printer and copier, the report may lose some of its visual impact. In this topic, you will learn a technique that enables you to distribute an Access report electronically to people who may not use Access. It also enables Access users to view a report without having to have access to the database in which it resides.

## Report Snapshot

### Definition:

A *report snapshot* is a file that contains an exact copy of an Access report. The snapshot will preserve all the objects contained within the report, such as the two-dimensional layout and the graphics.

### Example:

Figure 6-1 is an example of a report snapshot.

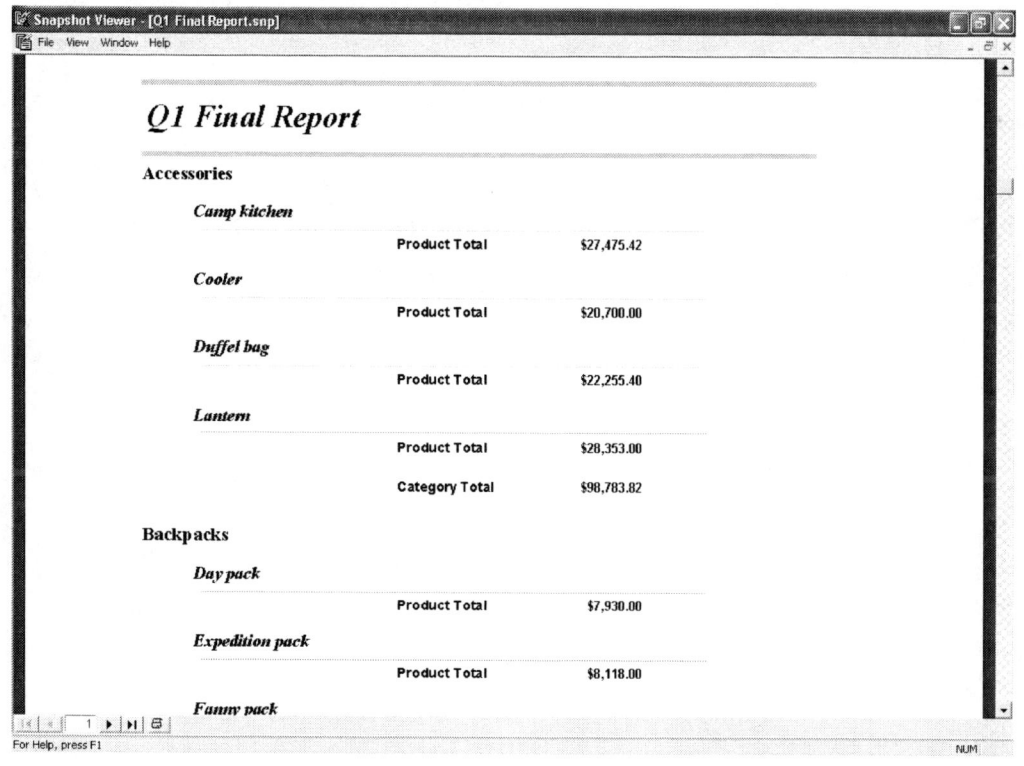

**Figure 6-1:** *A report snapshot.*

Lesson 6: Making Reports More Effective

# Lesson 6

## Snapshot Viewer

*Snapshot Viewer* is a program you can use to view and print an Access report snapshot. The viewer allows you to distribute your report to others who do not have Access installed on their computer.

## How to Create a Report Snapshot

### Procedure Reference: Create a Report Snapshot

To create a report snapshot:

1. In the Database window, select the report.
2. Choose File→Export.
3. Navigate to the storage location for the snapshot.
4. Enter a name for the snapshot file.
5. Open the Save As Type drop-down list and select Snapshot Format (*snp).
6. Click Export.

# ACTIVITY 6-4

## Creating a Snapshot

**Setup:**
Reports.mdb is open.

**Scenario:**
The president of the company has asked you to distribute the final sales report for the first quarter to all employees, but not all employees are Access users. So, you decide to try creating a report snapshot that you can embed in or attach to an email with instructions on downloading Snapshot Viewer.

# Lesson 6

| What You Do | How You Do It |
|---|---|
| 1. Preview both pages of the rptQ1Final report. Create a snapshot named *Q1 Final Report* and save it in the My Documents folder. | a. Preview both pages of rptQ1Final, and then close the report.<br><br>b. With rptQ1Final selected on the Reports tab, **choose File→Export**.<br><br>c. **Navigate to the My Documents folder.**<br><br>d. In the File Name text box, **type *Q1 Final Report***<br><br>e. From the Save As Type drop-down list, **select Snapshot Format (*.snp).**<br><br>f. **Select the Autostart option and click Export.** |
| 2. View both pages of the report in Snapshot Viewer. | a. View both pages of the report in Snapshot Viewer. |
| 3. Is the format of the report the same as it was displayed in Access? | |
| 4. Close Snapshot Viewer and the database. | a. Close Snapshot Viewer and the database. |

# Lesson 6 Follow-up

In this lesson, you made your reports more effective. Since reports are your main way of communicating database information with others, it is important that they be as effective as possible.

1. How will you improve your existing reports?

2. Can you think of any existing databases that could benefit from the use of columns? Explain.

*Lesson 6: Making Reports More Effective*

# Notes

# Lesson 7
# Maintaining an Access Database

**Lesson Time**
*30 minutes*

## Lesson Objectives:

In this lesson, you will maintain an Access database by using various utility tools.

You will:

- Link tables between Access databases.
- Back up a database from within Access.
- Compact and repair a database.
- Set a password on an Access database file.
- Use Object Dependency to determine which database objects rely on others.
- Document a database using the Database Documenter tool.
- Analyze the performance of a database.

# LESSON 7

## Introduction

Up until now, you have spent a majority of your time developing and customizing your database. Once the database is built, your major role will switch to maintenance. Database maintenance involves a new set of skills and tools provided by Access. In this lesson, you will use some of these tools to maintain an Access database.

A database is a growing, changing file that requires attention throughout its lifespan. Access provides a number of tools to keep your database performing optimally. Once you learn how to use them, database maintenance will be fast and simple.

# TOPIC A

## Link Tables to External Data Sources

If you look at any business, you will find that many data functions overlap from one department to another. This can cause many problems that range from conflicting information to outright errors in data. Linking tables to external data sources can solve this problem, reduce network load, and keep everyone up-to-date. In this topic, you will link a table to external data sources.

There is an old proverb warning against re-inventing the wheel. There really is no good reason to create a second copy of a database or spreadsheet if you need to use some of its data. As long as security options have been planned wisely, you can quickly grant permissions and link the information to your database. This will save you time, conserve network resources, and save you from duplicating data.

### Linking a File

*Linking a file* allows you to create a connection between your database and a separate file. This link allows you to display information from the separate file in your database. When linking a file, the link is dynamic and any changes that are made in the separate file will automatically be reflected in your database.

### How to Link Tables to External Data Sources

#### Procedure Reference: Link Tables

To link tables:

1. Open the database where you want the linked table to be.
2. Choose File→Get External Data→Link Tables.
3. Navigate to the database you want to link and double-click the file.
4. Select the database parts you want linked and click OK. The linked items will now show in the new database.

# ACTIVITY 7-1

## Linking a Table

### Data Files:
- Bob's Contacts.mdb
- Linking.mdb

### Scenario:
Your company has just acquired a new sales representative, and you have been commissioned to get his client contact list into the central contact database. Since he is always updating his contact list, you don't want to keep re-importing his information. You decide that linking to his table may be a better solution.

| What You Do | How You Do It |
|---|---|
| 1. From Linking.mdb, create a link to the Bob's Contacts table in Bob's Contacts.mdb. | a. Open Linking.mdb. |
| | b. Choose File→Get External Data→Link Tables. |
| | c. Navigate to Bob's Contacts.mdb and double-click the file. |
| | d. From the table list, **select Bob's Contacts and click OK.** The new table will now show on the Tables tab with a small arrow next to the table icon. |

**Lesson 7**

Lesson 7: Maintaining an Access Database

# Lesson 7

2. Open the linked table and examine the first record. In Bob's Contacts.mdb, change the company name of the first record to The Western Connection. Examine the effects on the linked table in Linking.mdb.

    a. Open the Bob's Contacts table.

    b. Examine the first record and close the table when finished.

    c. Open Bob's Contacts.mdb and open the Bob's Contacts table.

    d. Change the company name of the first record to *The Western Connection*

    Close the table when finished.

    e. Open Linking.mdb and open the Bob's Contacts linked table.

    f. Examine the company name of the first record. Close the table and database when finished.

3. True or False? When you made a change in the original table, the linked table was also updated.

    ___ True

    ___ False

# TOPIC B

# Back Up a Database

Database maintenance can be a full time job all by itself. One of the most important maintenance tasks is database backup. In this topic, you will back up a database.

You would never write a 200 page paper without bothering to save your work periodically. Forgetting to back up a database would be like doing just that. Performing regular backups ensures that if there ever is a problem, a minimal amount of data will be lost.

## How to Back Up a Database

### Procedure Reference: Back up a Database

To back up a database:

1. Open the database you wish to back up.

2. Choose File→Back Up Database.

3. Select the location for the backup, and name the file.

4. Click Save.

# ACTIVITY 7-2

## Backing Up a Database

### Data Files:

- Backing Up.mdb

### Scenario:

As your database grows, you realize that if it were somehow damaged there would be no way to recover all the data. In order to safeguard yourself against this, you decide to create a backup copy of your database.

| What You Do | How You Do It |
|---|---|
| 1. Create a backup copy of Backing Up.mdb on your desktop. Accept the default file name and close the database when done. | a. Open Backing Up.mdb.<br><br>b. Choose File→Back Up Database.<br><br>c. Navigate to the desktop and click Save, accepting the default file name.<br><br>d. Close the database when finished. |

2. What is added to the default file name when you back up a database?

   a) Time

   b) Date

   c) File Size

   d) Table Structure

3. Why might the date be a helpful addition to the file name when backing up databases?

*Lesson 7: Maintaining an Access Database*

**LESSON 7**

111

LESSON 7

## TOPIC C
# Compact and Repair a Database

As a database grows there are bound to be errors that spring up along the way. As the administrator of that database, you will be responsible for managing them. In this topic, you will compact and repair a database.

When errors occur in your database, they will take up room and slow down database performance. Compacting and repairing the database regularly will help keep errors and file size to a minimum, which will keep performance at a maximum.

## How to Compact and Repair a Database

**Procedure Reference: Compact and Repair a Database**

To compact and repair a database:

1.  Open the database you wish to compact and repair.
2.  Choose Tools→Database Utilities→Compact And Repair Database.

# ACTIVITY 7-3

## Compacting a Database

**Data Files:**

- Compact.mdb

**Scenario:**

You have finally finished all your work on a new database and you're ready to hand it off to a co-worker. The last step in doing a professional job is to clean up the database so it will run as efficiently as possible. You'll do this by using the Compact And Repair utility.

| What You Do | How You Do It |
| --- | --- |
| 1. Using Windows Explorer, **navigate to the folder containing Compact.mdb and make a note of the size of the file.** | a. **Right-click the Start menu and choose Explore.** <br><br> b. **Navigate to the folder containing Compact.mdb.** <br><br> c. **Choose View→Details** to view file sizes. <br><br> d. **Note the size of Compact.mdb** _____ . |

112     Microsoft® Office Access 2003: Level 3

2. In Access, **run the Compact And Repair utility on Compact.mdb.** In Windows Explorer, view and make a note of the size of Compact.mdb. Then, close Windows Explorer and Compact.mdb.

   a. Open Contact.mdb.

   b. From the Access file menu, **choose Tools→Database Utilities→Compact And Repair Database.**

   c. Note the new size of Compact.mdb.

   d. Close Windows Explorer.

   e. Close Compact.mdb.

3. What happened to the file size after you ran the Compact And Repair utility?

# TOPIC D

# Protect a Database with a Password

Many times, a database will contain information that you do not want available to everyone. Requiring a password can solve this problem. In this topic, you will protect a database with a password.

In order to protect your valuables, you might put them in a safe that only you know the combination to. The same is true of a database. You can protect the information inside by requiring the user to provide a password before they can see what's inside.

## How to Protect a Database with a Password

### Procedure Reference: Password Protect a Database

To password protect a database:

1. With Access already running, choose File→Open.
2. Highlight the database you want to password protect.
3. Click the down arrow next to the Open button and choose Open Exclusive.
4. Choose Tools→Security→Set Database Password.
5. Type the same password in the Password and Verify text boxes.
6. Click OK.

*Lesson 7: Maintaining an Access Database*

# Lesson 7

# ACTIVITY 7-4

## Password Protecting a Database

### Data Files:

- Password Protect.mdb

### Scenario:

Management is becoming concerned with who has access to the company database. They decide that you must password protect the database so only those who know the password can gain access. The password they want you to use is "money."

# LESSON 7

| What You Do | How You Do It |
|---|---|
| 1. Open Password Protect.mdb exclusively and set the password to money. | a. With Access already running, **choose File→Open**. |
| | b. **Navigate to the folder containing Password Protect.mdb and highlight it.** |
| | c. **Click the down arrow to the right of the Open button and choose Open Exclusive.** |
| 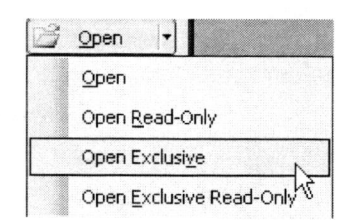 | d. With Password Protect.mdb now open exclusively, **choose Tools→Security→Set Database Password**. |
| | e. In the Set Database Password box, **type *money* in both the Password and Verify text boxes**. |
| 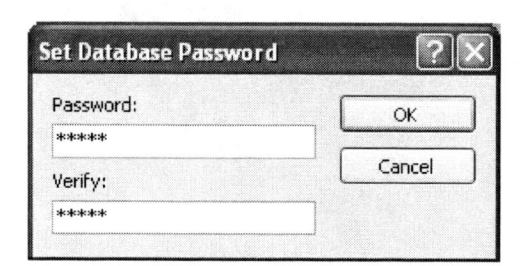 | **Click OK.** |
| 2. Close the database and reopen it to verify that it requires a password. Type the new password to gain access to the database. Close the database when finished. | a. **Close the database.** |
| | b. **Navigate to the folder containing Password Protect.mdb and double-click the file.** |
| | c. When prompted for a password, **type *money* and click OK**. |
| | d. **Close the database when finished.** |

*Lesson 7: Maintaining an Access Database*

# LESSON 7

## TOPIC E

# Determine Object Dependency

As you build a database, the tables and queries inside are intertwined and dependant on each other in order to function properly. Therefore, when you make a change to the database, the effects go beyond just the table or query where the change was made. The Object Dependency task pane will allow you to view the relationships between the objects in a database before you make any changes. In this topic, you will determine object dependency.

Understanding the relationship between all the pieces of a database can be very helpful when troubleshooting a problem. The Object Dependency task pane will allow you to see the relationship between different segments of your database.

## Object Dependency Task Pane

The *Object Dependency task pane* allows you to examine the objects in your database and see how they work with each other. Before moving or deleting an object you would want to check the Object Dependency task pane to see what other objects would be affected by the change.

## How to Determine Object Dependency

### Procedure Reference: Determine Object Dependency

To determine object dependency:

1. Right-click the item whose object dependency you want to check.
2. Choose Object Dependency from the drop-down menu.
3. By default, the task pane will show objects that depend on that item. To see the objects that item depends on, select the Objects That I Depend On option.

# ACTIVITY 7-5

## Determining Object Dependency

**Data Files:**

- Dependencies.mdb

**Scenario:**

Management has requested that you go through the company database and clean up any queries that are no longer useful. The first query in question is the qselOrders query. Before anything gets deleted, you want to check and see if other portions of the database will be affected by its removal.

| What You Do | How You Do It |
|---|---|
| 1. In Dependencies.mdb, open the Object Dependencies task pane for the qselOrders query. | a. Open Dependencies.mdb.<br><br>b. From the Queries tab, **right-click qselOrders.**<br><br>c. **Choose Object Dependencies from the list.** The Object Dependencies task pane will appear on the right side of the window.<br><br>d. If necessary, **click OK to close the window.** |
| 2. Explore the object dependency for qselOrders. Check both the items that depend on the query, and the items the query depends upon. Close the database when finished. | a. Note that qselCustExtend query is dependent on qselOrders. Deleting this query would cause qselCustExtend to malfunction as well. **Select the Objects That I Depend On option.**<br><br>b. Note that the qselOrders query draws information from four different tables. **Close the database when finished.** |

*Lesson 7: Maintaining an Access Database*

# LESSON 7

## TOPIC F

# Document a Database

After a database is created, it is always a good idea to have documentation to support it. The Database Documenter tool can help you with this process. In this topic, you will document a database.

Even though everything in a database you created makes perfect sense to you, others might not completely understand what your intentions are for certain areas. Having good documentation can help to alleviate most of this confusion. For example, when you are on vacation, someone has to fill in for you and maintain that database. If there is no documentation for them to reference, they could run into problems.

## Database Documenter

The *Database Documenter* allows you to create a report about all the objects in your database. You can control the level of detail that is reported by documenting only the objects that are important to you.

## How to Document a Database

### Procedure Reference: Use the Database Documenter Tool

To use the Database Documenter tool:

1. Open the database you want to document.
2. Choose Tools→Analyze→Documenter.
3. Select the objects on which you want to create documentation.
4. Click OK.

# ACTIVITY 7-6

## Using the Database Documenter Tool

### Data Files:
- Documenter.mdb

### Scenario:
Your company has just hired a new database administrator to help you manage the company database. Before they arrive you take the time to create documentation on the database so that they will have some reference material. Instead of attempting to make something from scratch, you use Access' Database Documenter tool to create the documentation for you.

| What You Do | How You Do It |
|---|---|
| 1. From Documenter.mdb, **start the Database Documenter Wizard.** | a. **Open Documenter.mdb.** <br><br> b. **Choose Tools→Analyze→Documenter.** |
| 2. From the Documenter Wizard, **create documentation for all object types in the database.** | a. From the Documenter Wizard, **click the All Object Types tab.** <br><br> b. **Click Select All.** <br><br> c. **Click OK** to create the documentation. |
| 3. **Examine the documentation created by the Database Documenter. Save and close the database when finished.** | a. **Zoom in and page through the documentation.** <br><br> b. **Close the database.** |

*Lesson 7: Maintaining an Access Database*

# LESSON 7

# TOPIC G

## Analyze the Performance of a Database

Once a database is in use, you will need to monitor its performance. Access provides you with a Performance Analyzer tool to help you to that end. In this topic, you will analyze the performance of a database.

Monitoring the performance of a database will allow you to keep a close lookout for any problems that might occur. If you notice a sharp drop in performance, you can investigate further and take care of the situation quickly before anyone even notices. Without this tool, you wouldn't be aware of these issues until they were reported to you by a user.

### Performance Analyzer

The *Performance Analyzer* evaluates your database for efficiency. It will also create a suggestion list of things you can change to improve database performance.

### How to Analyze the Performance of a Database

**Procedure Reference: Analyze Database Performance**

To analyze database performance:

1. Open the database you want to analyze.
2. Choose Tools→Analyze→Performance.
3. Select the objects that you want to analyze.
4. Click OK.

# ACTIVITY 7-7

## Analyzing the Performance of a Database

**Data Files:**

- Performance.mdb

**Scenario:**

One of your co-workers has been doing some work on a side project. They ask you if you can take a look at their database and see if you can spot any ways that can improve its performance. The first thing you want to do is run the Performance Analyzer.

| What You Do | How You Do It |
|---|---|
| 1. From Performance.mdb, **start the Performance Analyzer Wizard.** | a. **Open Performance.mdb.**<br><br>b. **Choose Tools→Analyze→Performance.** |
| 2. From the Performance Analyzer Wizard, **analyze the performance for all object types in the database. Save and close the database when finished.** | a. From the Performance Analyzer Wizard, **click the All Object Types tab.**<br><br>b. **Click Select All.**<br><br>c. **Click OK** to run the Analyzer.<br><br>d. **Click through the Analysis results, reading the suggestions given in the Analysis Notes section.**<br><br>e. **Close the Performance Analyzer Wizard.**<br><br>f. **Close the database.** |

# Lesson 7 Follow-up

In this lesson, you maintained an Access database. Using the tools that Access provides, you can effectively manage your database over its entire life span.

1. **Are there any maintenance techniques that you haven't been using that you will start using now? Explain.**

2. **What maintenance tools do you think will be most useful for your job? Why?**

*Lesson 7: Maintaining an Access Database*

# FOLLOW-UP

# Follow-up

In this course, you improved your existing databases by employing many new tools and techniques. You are now able to turn your simple databases into robust, highly efficient databases. This makes both your job, and that of your end user, much easier.

1. **Are there any mistakes you have been making with your existing databases? How will you fix them?**

2. **After taking this course, what things might you want to change about your existing databases?**

3. **What concepts were you unaware of before this course?**

## What's Next?

Completing this course has prepared you to take the next course in this series, which is *Microsoft® Office Access 2003: Level 4.*

# APPENDIX A
# Microsoft Office Specialist Program

Selected Element K courseware addresses Microsoft Office Specialist skills. The following tables indicate where Access 2003 skills are covered. For example, 1-3 indicates the lesson and activity number applicable to that skill.

| Core Skill Sets and Skills Being Measured | Access 2003: Level 1 | Access 2003: Level 2 | Access 2003: Level 3 | Access 2003: Level 4 |
|---|---|---|---|---|
| Create Access Databases | | | | |
| Creating databases using Database Wizard | | 2-1 | | |
| Creating blank databases | | 2-2 | | |
| Create and Modify Tables | | | | |
| Creating tables using Table Wizard | | 2-3 | | |
| Modifying table properties or structure | | 2-4, 2-5, 2-6, 3-1 | | |
| Define and Modify Field Types | | | | |
| Creating Lookup fields | | 3-3 | | |
| Changing field types | | 2-5 | | |
| Modify Field Properties | | | | |
| Changing field properties to display input masks | | 3-2 | | |
| Modify field properties for tables in Table Design view | | 3-1 | | |
| Create and Modify One-to-many Relationships | | | | |
| Creating and modifying one-to-many relationships | | 2-7 | | |
| Enforce Referential Integrity | | | | |
| Enforcing referential integrity in a one-to-many relationship | | 2-7 | | |

# APPENDIX A

| Core Skill Sets and Skills Being Measured | Access 2003: Level 1 | Access 2003: Level 2 | Access 2003: Level 3 | Access 2003: Level 4 |
|---|---|---|---|---|
| Create and Modify Queries | | | | |
| Creating and modifying Select queries using the Simple Query Wizard | 4-3 | | | |
| Creating and modifying Crosstab, unmatched and duplicates queries | | | 2-1, 2-3 | |
| Create Forms | | | | |
| Creating forms using the Form Wizard | 5-3 | | | |
| Creating auto forms | 5-2 | | | |
| Add and Modify Form Controls and Properties | | | | |
| Modifying form properties | 5-5, 5-6, 5-7, 5-8 | | | |
| Modifying specific form controls (e.g., text boxes, labels, bound controls) | 5-5, 5-6, 6-5 | 6-1 | | |
| Create Reports | | | | |
| Creating reports | 6-1, 6-2 | 7-1, 7-6 | | |
| Add and Modify Report Control Properties | | | | |
| Adding calculated controls to a report selection | 6-4 | 7-4 | | |
| Create a Data Access Page | | | | |
| Creating data access pages using the Page Wizard | | | | 1-1 |
| Enter, Edit, and Delete Records | | | | |
| Entering records into a datasheet | 2-2 | | | |
| Find and Move Among Records | | | | |
| Using navigation controls to move among records | 2-1, 2-5 | | | |
| Import Data to Access | | | | |
| Importing structured data into tables | | | 3-4 | |
| Create and Modify Calculated Fields and Aggregate Functions | | | | |
| Adding calculated fields to queries in Query Design View | 4-5 | | | |
| Using aggregate functions in queries (e.g., AVG, COUNT) | 4-6 | | | |
| Modify Form Layout | | | | |
| Aligning and spacing controls | 5-6, 5-7 | | | |
| Showing and hiding headers and footers | | 6-1 | | |

# Appendix A

| Core Skill Sets and Skills Being Measured | Access 2003: Level 1 | Access 2003: Level 2 | Access 2003: Level 3 | Access 2003: Level 4 |
|---|---|---|---|---|
| Modify Report Layout and Page Setup | | | | |
| Changing margins and page orientation | | 7-5 | | |
| Aligning, resizing, and spacing controls | | 7-3 | | |
| Format Datasheets | | | | |
| Formatting a table or query for display | | | 1-4 | |
| Sort Records | | | | |
| Sorting records in tables, queries, forms, and reports | 2-3 | 5-1, 7-1 | | |
| Filter Records | | | | |
| Filtering datasheets by form | | 4-1 | | |
| Filtering datasheets by selection | 2-4 | 4-1 | | |
| Identify Object Dependencies | | | | |
| Identify object dependencies | | | 7-5 | |
| View Objects and Object Data in Other Views | | | | |
| Previewing for print | | 2-7 | | |
| Using datasheet, PivotChart, Web page and layout view | 1-4 | | 2-5 | 1-1, 1-3, 2-5 |
| Print Database Objects and Data | | | | |
| Printing database objects and data | | 2-7 | 1-4 | |
| Export Data From Access | | | | |
| Exporting data from Access (e.g., Excel) | | 8-3 | | |
| Back Up a Database | | | | |
| Backing up a database | | | 7-2 | |
| Compact and Repair Databases | | | | |
| Using Compact and Repair | | | 7-3 | |

*Appendix A: Microsoft Office Specialist Program*

# Notes

# LESSON LABS

Due to classroom setup constraints, some labs cannot be keyed in sequence immediately following their associated lesson. Your instructor will tell you whether your labs can be practiced immediately following the lesson or whether they require separate setup from the main lesson content.

# LESSON 1 LAB 1

## Putting Existing Data into Correctly Designed Tables

### Data Files:
- CompanyCentral.mdb

### Scenario:
The human resources manager at your company asks you to look at a table in his CompanyCentral database that he has been using to keep track of employee data. From your initial look at the database, you can tell you will need new tables for employees and health plans. You also want to make sure that you go back and clean up any tables that are no longer used when you're done.

1. In CompanyCentral.mdb, **open the CompanyEmployees table** to see if there are any problems with the table design.

2. **Close the table and run the Table Analyzer Wizard up to the point where the wizard has grouped the data into tables.**

3. The wizard has grouped the Health-related data into table 2. The State field is out of place there. **Drag the State field back to table 1** (between City and Zip).

4. Rename table 1 as *tblEmployees*.

   Rename table 2 as *tblHealthPlan*.

5. **Complete the wizard. Review the results and then close the tables.**

# LESSON LABS

6. Delete the CompanyEmployees_OLD table from the database.

7. Close the CompanyCentral database.

# LESSON 2 LAB 1

## Summarizing Data

**Data Files:**

- MusicCentral.mdb

**Scenario:**

The Music Shop is a large musical instrument manufacturing company. The Training Center regularly offers courses to Music Shop employees. In the MusicCentral database, you keep track of the courses offered and employees who have registered for the courses. Rather than seeing lengthy registration lists, you want to be able to summarize data that is contained in these tables. For instance, you want to view, in a single table, the names of students and the number of courses for which they've registered, calculated by course type. You would also like to create a PivotTable view of the StudentCourses query. This will enable you to look at the count of students in each class and manipulate the class codes and start dates to expand or confine the display.

> In the MusicCentral database, the queries qselSolutionStudentCourses_Crosstab and qselSolutionStudentCourses are the completed files of this activity. You can compare your results to these queries.

1. In the MusicCentral database, **familiarize yourself with the design of qselStudentCourses.** This query combines data from four separate tables. **Close the query.**

2. Start the Crosstab Query Wizard and base the new query on qselStudentCourses.

3. Designate the values in the StudentName field as row headings.

4. Select the values in the TypeCode field to be column headings.

5. Display a count of course codes for which students are registered as values.

6. Name the query *qselStudentCourses_Crosstab*

7. Save the query and close the datasheet.

128  Microsoft® Office Access 2003: Level 3

8. **Open the StudentCourses query and create a PivotTable view with the following parameters:**
   - The TypeCode is a Filter.
   - The StartDate as Rows.
   - The CourseCode field as Columns.
   - Designate the StudentID field as a Sum calculation and hide the details in PivotTable view.

9. **Use the TypeCode drop-down list to confine the view to courses of a certain type.**

10. When you're done, **display all of the TypeCodes.**

11. **Close the window, saving changes to the layout. Close the database.**

# Lesson 3 Lab 1

## Creating a Basic Access Macro to Display a Form

### Data Files:
- HealthCentral.mdb
- SolutionHealthCentral.mdb

### Scenario:
Currently, primary employee data is accessed through the EmployeeData form, but the Health Plan options are accessed through another form, frmHealthData. HR personnel could be more efficient if they could access the health plan information for an employee right from the main form.

*The SolutionHealthCentral database is a completed file of this activity. You can compare your results to this database.*

1. In the HealthCentral database, **create a macro named *mfrmMyHealthPlan* that will:**
   - Set the Echo Action to Off.
   - Open the frmHealthData form.
   - Set the Where condition to `[HealthCode]=[Forms]![frmEmployeeData]![HealthCode]`

2. **Open frmEmployeeData.**

# LESSON LABS

3. With the Control Wizards tool deactivated, **create a command button named** *HealthPlan*.

   **Attach the mfrmMyHealthPlan macro to the On Click Event property of the command button.**

4. **Save the form.**

5. **Test the Health Plan command button.**

6. **Close the forms and the HealthCentral database.**

# LESSON 4 LAB 1

## Creating a Macro that Requires Data Entry

### Data Files:

- DepartmentCentral.mdb

### Scenario:

Your primary employee data is accessed through the EmployeeData form. Sometimes, when entering a new employee record, the Dept field is left blank, which only complicates things later on. HR personnel could be more efficient if an entry was required in the Dept field.

> In the DepartmentCentral database, frmSolutionEmployeeData and mcrSolutionMyPracticeDept are the end results of this activity. You can compare your results to this form and the macro associated with it.

1. In the DepartmentCentral database, **open frmEmployeeData.** This form is based on the EmployeeData query.

2. **Save the form as** *frmMyEmployeeData*.

3. In the form's Design view, **attach a new macro, mfrmMyPracticeDept, to the form's Before Update property. Use the Macro Builder to create a macro named** *mfrmMyPracticeDept*. **The macro should perform the following actions:**
   - Check that a value has been entered into the Dept field.
   - Not allow the record to be saved to the table if the Dept field is blank.
   - Inform the user that the Dept field must contain a value.
   - Move the insertion point to the Dept field.

4. **Review the macro to be sure you have included all necessary arguments.**

5. Test the macro.

6. Close the form and the DepartmentCentral database.

# LESSON 5 LAB 1

## Enhancing a Form

### Data Files:

- BookCentral.mdb

### Scenario:

The BookCentral database stores information for the Canal House Books publishing company. You've been given the task of creating a form for sales reps that they can fill out when a new customer places an order. It should include customer and billing information, and it should effectively facilitate data entry. You've got the file started, but the company has made a few requests:

- A Tab control to organize customer and billing information.
- Highlight any customer that has joined the company since the start of 2000.
- A calendar on the form to assist with questions regarding billing cycles.

*In the BookCentral database, frmSolutionCustomerInformation is a completed file of this activity. You can compare your results to this form.*

1. In the BookCentral database, **open frmCustomerInformation.**

2. To organize basic customer information and customer billing information, **add a Tab control to the Detail section of the form by clicking in the upper-left corner of the form.**

3. Change the name of the top page to *Customer Information*.

   Add the following fields in an appropriate arrangement: CustomerID, CustomerName, Address, City, Region, Country, PostalCode, Phone, and Fax.

4. Change the name of the second page to *Billing Information*.

   Add the following fields in an appropriate arrangement: Salesperson, ContactLastName, ContactFirstName, FirstOrder, and BillAccount.

5. Apply conditional formatting to the FirstOrder text box control on this form. Values greater than 1/1/2000 should be displayed in bold with a blue fill color.

# LESSON LABS

6. On the Billing Information page, **add an ActiveX Calendar Control and adjust its size.**

7. **Save the form as *frmMyCustomerInformation*.**

8. **View the form in Form view and input a sample record to test your form.**

   *You might want to input one record, and then make additional changes based on how easy it was to input the first record.*

9. **Close the form and the BookCentral database.**

# LESSON 6 LAB 1

## Enhancing a Report

**Data Files:**

- GourmetCentral.mdb

**Scenario:**

You work at The Gourmet Shop. Your boss wants to look more closely at orders for each company sales rep. You have created a report, called rptCustomerOrders, that prints a report for the sales rep and month of your choice; however, sometimes an incorrect sales rep number is entered and the report detail is blank. In that event, you want to cancel the printing of a blank report by using the mcrNoData macro that you've created. In addition, you want to enhance the report by adding a chart as part of your printed output, to make the sales results for each rep more obvious. You want the chart to show the total for each sales rep, so you created qtotRep to produce that data. Finally, you need to distribute this report to several co-workers, not all of whom use Access.

*In the GourmetCentral database, rptSolutionCustomerOrders is a completed file of this activity. You can compare your results to this report.*

1. In the GourmetCentral database, **open rptCustomerOrders. Preview the report for sales rep 2 for the state of MN. Next, preview the report for sales rep 2 in the state of NY. Review the content of the report and then switch to Design view.**

2. You've created and stored a macro, mcrNoData, that cancels printing when the report doesn't contain detail records. **Set the report's On No Data event property to this macro. Using the same combinations as in step 1, test to see if the macro works as intended.**

3. Use the Chart Wizard to add a chart to your report. Insert the chart in the Report Footer, basing the chart on the qtotRep query. Add both fields and select a 3-D Column chart. The chart should be laid out with the Rep along the bottom axis and the Total Sales along the left. Choose not to have the chart change from record to record and do not include a legend. Assign the chart a title of *Sales Rep Figures*.

4. Create a report for sales rep 1 for the state of FL. Create a report snapshot and then view the report in Snapshot Viewer.

5. Close the GourmetCentral database.

# LESSON 7 LAB 1

## Maintaining a Database

### Data Files:

- LonePine.mdb

### Scenario:

Now that you have completed work on the LonePine.mdb database, you will be moving on to another project. Before your work is complete, there are a few last tasks the company has requested from you:

- Create a backup copy of the database in its current state.
- Password protect the database with a password of Camping.
- Create documentation for the entire database.
- Make the database file size as small as possible.

1. From LonePine.mdb, **add a password of Camping to the database. Test that the password is working by closing and re-opening the database.**

2. **Run the Database Documenter utility to create documentation for all parts of the database.** The resulting report could be printed and kept as hard copy documentation for the database.

3. **Run the Compact And Repair utility. Check the file size before and after the operation to view the decrease in size.**

4. **Create a backup copy of the database and save it to the My Documents folder. Use the default naming convention.**

# Lesson Labs

5. **Save and close the database.**

# SOLUTIONS

## Activity 1-2

2. **What is the major problem with the data caused by a poor table design?**

   *Many fields contain repeated data, making searches difficult and data maintenance inaccurate.*

3. **What is the cause of these problems?**

   *The table contains too many fields.*

4. **What is the cure for these problems?**

   *Break the data into multiple tables.*

6. **Do you agree with the way the wizard has grouped the data into tables?**

   *The groupings of the data seem appropriate. Table1 has the details of each order, Table2 has order data, Table3 has data specific to each product, Table4 has customer data, and Table5 has product categories.*

8. **Do you agree with the primary key fields identified by the wizard? If necessary, refer to the original data.**

   *The wizard correctly identified the OrderNum and CustomerNum fields as primary key fields for their respective tables. Given the lack of other unique identifying fields in the original data, the wizard will add AutoNumber ID fields as primary keys for the other tables.*

10. **Have the data problems been eliminated?**

    *Yes. Each table has an appropriate primary key and the unnecessarily repeated data is no longer present.*

11. **Is there anything in the design of some of the tables that you are not used to seeing in your own tables?**

    *The foreign key fields contain more than one value.*

## Activity 1-3

3. **Why can't Access append all the records?**

   *Because tblEmployees has duplicate records in the EmployeeID and ProjectNum fields. These fields are the primary key of tblAssignments, so they can't contain duplicate records. This behavior eliminates the duplicate records in the new table by discarding the duplicates.*

## Activity 2-2

2. **What are the groupings of records?**

   *Records are grouped first on Customer Name and then on Product.*

# SOLUTIONS

4. **What is the purpose of the calculated expression?**

    *The expression creates a calculated field named TotalSales. It multiplies the Quantity and Price values, formats the result as currency, and then totals the result for each group of products.*

## Activity 2-3

4. **What are the features of the resulting datasheet?**
    - *Products are listed in alphabetical order within each category.*
    - *A Total Of Sale field is displayed.*
    - *The total sales for each product for the months of January, February, and March are displayed.*
    - *There are blank columns for the remaining months of the year.*
    - *There are 16 records.*

6. **What features do you notice in the design created by the wizard?**
    - *The Crosstab Query Wizard created a totals query that also has a crosstab row.*
    - *Each field is designated as a Row Heading, Column Heading, or a Value.*
    - *The Date values are formatted as the three-letter abbreviation for the month and are grouped on that value.*

## Activity 2-4

1. **What is the name of the wizard you can use to create a crosstab query?**

    a) Crosstab Wizard

    ✓ b) Crosstab Query Wizard

    c) Crosstab Filter Query Wizard

    d) Crosstab Filter Wizard

2. **Which of the following are true of creating crosstab queries with the Crosstab Query Wizard?**

    a) The result is a query that sorts data.

    b) The calculation used must be based on numeric data, and not on date datatypes.

    ✓ c) You can choose what data will be displayed for the row and column headings and how the intersecting data will be calculated.

    d) The data calculation can only be a sum or an average.

## Activity 2-7

7. **What data does the PivotChart show as you move through the records?**

    *It shows the data only for the customer displayed in the main form.*

# SOLUTIONS

## Activity 3-2

3. **When do you want the macro to execute?**

   *When the button is clicked.*

4. **To what event should the macro be attached?**

   *The On Click event.*

# Lesson 4

## Activity 4-1

1. **What action by the user should trigger this macro?**

   *User tries to save a record with a blank CustomerName field.*

2. **What is the first thing the macro should do?**

   *Cancel saving the record.*

3. **What is the second thing the macro should do?**

   *Alert the user with a message box, telling them that they must add information to the CustomerName field.*

4. **What is the third thing the macro should do?**

   *Move the insertion point to the CustomerName field.*

5. **Which control can trigger this macro?**

   *The Form object.*

6. **Which event property can trigger this macro when you need to use it?**

   *The Before Update property.*

7. **When will you want this macro to run?**

   *Only when a certain condition exists: When the CustomerName field is empty.*

## Activity 4-2

8. **What happens when you try to advance to a new record?**

   *You are unable to save the new record. The record you just entered is still displayed, as is the pencil icon. The insertion point is in the CustomerName field. Because the condition is True (the field is empty), the macro carried out the macro actions.*

10. **A dialog box indicates that you are unable to save the new record. Why?**

    *Access has evaluated the expression in the Condition column. Since there is no value in the CustomerName field, Access prevents you from saving the record.*

# SOLUTIONS

## Activity 5-2

3. What other changes might you want to make to the appearance of the form or the calendar?

   *Other changes may include:*
   - *additional sizing of the control or the form;*
   - *displaying the full name of the month; and*
   - *not having the current date selected.*

## Activity 5-3

1. How might you categorize the data in the qselEmployeeInfo query?

   *The data can be categorized into personal information (home address and phone) and company-related information such as pay rate, department, and whether or not the person is enrolled in the health plan.*

## Activity 6-3

6. If your report is not on one page, what are some techniques you can use to make it more compact?

   *You could decrease the top and bottom margins. You could decrease font sizes and/or the height of various sections.*

## Activity 6-4

3. Is the format of the report the same as it was displayed in Access?

   *Yes, the report looks the same as in Access.*

# Lesson 7

## Activity 7-1

3. True or False? When you made a change in the original table, the linked table was also updated.

   ✓ True
   ___ False

# Activity 7-2

2. What is added to the default file name when you back up a database?

    a) Time

    ✓ b) Date

    c) File Size

    d) Table Structure

3. Why might the date be a helpful addition to the file name when backing up databases?

    *If there were several backup copies, you would be able to tell when each of them were created.*

# Activity 7-3

3. What happened to the file size after you ran the Compact And Repair utility?

    *The file size decreased.*

# Notes

# Glossary

**conditional formatting**
An Access tool that enables you to change the formatting of a control based on conditions that you define.

**Criteria field**
A field that allows you to apply conditions to your queries. You can limit the records returned by a query to only those that meet specific requirements that you declare.

**crosstab query**
A query that calculates and summarizes table data. Using the Crosstab Query Wizard, the user can choose what data will be displayed for the row and column headings, and how the intersecting data is calculated.

**Database Documenter**
Allows you to create a report about any or all the objects in your database.

**Duplicates query**
Checks a table for duplicate records.

**form**
An interface used to interact with a database. The form creator can completely customize the form to the needs of the database.

**imported data**
External information that can be brought into and used in an Access database.

**junction table**
A table that eliminates a many-to-many relationship between two other tables.

**linking a file**
Allows you to create a connection between your database and a separate file. When linking a file, the link is dynamic and any changes that are made in the separate file will automatically be reflected in your database.

**macro**
An Access object that consists of a series of actions that are automatically performed for you. You can create a macro to automate a process or a series of tasks.

**macro condition**
An expression that enables a macro to perform certain tasks only if a specific situation exists.

**Macro window**
The interface in which macros are created.

**many-to-many relationship**
An association between two Access tables where multiple records in one table can correspond to multiple records in the other table.

**message box**
A small window that can appear to prompt the user or give them information.

**Object Dependency task pane**
Allows you to examine the objects in your database and see how they work with each other.

**object event**
An action that is caused by the user.

**Performance Analyzer**
Evaluates your database for efficiency. It will also create a suggestion list of things you can change to improve database performance.

# GLOSSARY

**PivotChart**
A database view that shows a graphical analysis of data in a datasheet or form.

**PivotTable**
A database view that allows you to summarize and examine data in a datasheet or form.

**primary key**
A field or combination of fields in a table that uniquely identifies each record in a table.

**report**
An Access tool that allows you to concisely display database information that will be valuable to others. Reports may be distributed electronically or printed.

**report snapshot**
A file that contains an exact copy of an Access report.

**Snapshot Viewer**
A program that is used to view and print an Access report snapshot.

**tab pages**
An Access control that allows you to create multiple pages on one form. Each page is separated by its own tab.

**table**
A structured collection of data on a specific topic. Data is organized into columns and rows.

**Table Analyzer Wizard**
A tool that helps manage an existing Access database by suggesting how to make it run more efficiently.

**unmatched query**
Compares two tables and displays the records that are not duplicated in both tables.

**Where condition**
An argument that can be used to compare and restrict the records that are displayed on two related forms.

# INDEX

## A
adding charts, 95
automating data entry, 68

## B
backing up databases, 110
BorderStyle settings, 79

## C
calendars
  displaying, 80
cancel a report, 92
Chart Wizard, 95
charts
  adding to reports, 95
columns
  hiding, 13
common event properties, 58
conditional formatting, 76
  applying, 76
Criteria fields, 23, 24
crosstab queries, 27, 28
Crosstab Query Wizard, 27

## D
data
  importing, 3
  printing in columns, 99
  summarizing, 24
data entry
  automating, 68
  condition, 68
  events, 69
  requiring with a macro, 61
Database Documenter, 118
  using, 118
database performance
  analyzing, 120
databases
  adding passwords, 113
  backing up, 110
  compacting and repairing, 112
  documenting, 118
duplicate records
  finding, 20
Duplicates queries, 20
  creating, 20

## E
event properties for data entry, 69
expressions
  entering in a macro argument, 54

## F
files
  linking, 108
form properties, 79
forms, 39
  creating a PivotChart on, 39
  creating new, 85
  properties, 79

## I
imported data, 2

## J
junction tables, 10
  adding existing data, 11
  creating, 11

## L
linking a file, 108
linking tables, 108

## M
macro arguments, 54
macro conditions, 58
Macro window, 46
macros, 46

*Index*     **143**

# INDEX

attaching to command buttons, 51
creating, 46, 47
creating to open a form, 48
modifying to display a message box, 66
planning, 59
requiring data entry, 61
types, 61
using to cancel a report, 92
many-to-many relationships, 10
message boxes, 66
  displaying, 66

## O

object dependency
  determining, 116
Object Dependency task pane, 116
object events, 50
  categories, 50

## P

passwords, 113
Performance Analyzer, 120
PivotCharts, 32, 40
  creating, 33
  using on forms, 39
  working with, 37
PivotTables, 32
  creating, 33
primary keys, 10

## R

records
  restricting, 53
repairing a database, 112
report events, 92
report snapshots, 103
  creating, 104
reports, 92
  cancelling, 92
  creating, 98
  multiple-column reports
  multiple-column, 98
restricting records, 53

## S

Snapshot Viewer, 104

## T

tab pages, 85
  definition of, 85

using to create new forms, 85
Table Analyzer Wizard, 5
  using, 6
table columns
  hiding, 13
table structure
  improving, 13
tables, 2
  analyzing, 6
  linking, 108
  restructuring, 13

## U

unmatched queries, 20
  creating, 20
using to summarize data, 24, 28

## W

Where condition, 53
  using to restrict records, 53